BLUE COLLAR MENTALITY

BLUE COLLAR MENTALITY

BOISE STATE'S RISE TO FOOTBALL PROMINENCE

TOM BARBOUR

Tate Publishing & *Enterprises*

Blue Collar Mentality
Copyright © 2009 by Tom Barbour. All rights reserved.

No part of this publication may be reproduced, stored in a retrieval system or transmitted in any way by any means, electronic, mechanical, photocopy, recording or otherwise without the prior permission of the author except as provided by USA copyright law.

The opinions expressed by the author are not necessarily those of Tate Publishing, LLC.

Published by Tate Publishing & Enterprises, LLC
127 E. Trade Center Terrace | Mustang, Oklahoma 73064 USA
1.888.361.9473 | www.tatepublishing.com

Tate Publishing is committed to excellence in the publishing industry. The company reflects the philosophy established by the founders, based on Psalm 68:11,
"The Lord gave the word and great was the company of those who published it."

Book design copyright © 2009 by Tate Publishing, LLC. All rights reserved.
Cover design by Lance Waldrop
Interior design by Jeff Fisher

Published in the United States of America

ISBN:978-1-61566-422-1
1. Sports & Recreation, Football
2. Sports & Recreation, History
09.11.23

"We do not take counsel of our fears, our naysayers or the unknown."

—Chris Petersen
Boise State Head Football Coach

DEDICATION

To my father, Robert Duke Barbour, Jr., the best high school basketball and football player in the state of Idaho, 1941–1942.

ACKNOWLEDGMENTS

A special thanks to former defensive tackle Tony Altieri for his invaluable perspective on the early D-I years. If one could choose a poster child to represent Boise State football for the past ten years, it might be Tony. We actually met by complete happenstance (or probably more accurately, divine appointment) in church one Sunday shortly after he moved back to Southern California from Boise. The hours we spent on Saturday mornings at Starbucks seemed to fly by much too quickly.

Another former defensive tackle and current director of the Boise State Varsity B Club, Michel

Bourgeau, could not have been more helpful. Michel, who is one of the all-time great Bronco players and a member of the 1980 national championship team, was instrumental in providing contact information for many of the people to whom I talked at Boise State, including former players.

Dr. Jim DeSaegher, UCLA Bruin, Point Loma University English professor extraordinaire, and long-time friend, was beyond gracious to take his time to give editing input. My lovely wife of twenty-eight years also lent her sharp detail mind to correct my sometimes strange sentence structure and punctuation.

The guys that are even older than I am added spice to my research. Former Boise Junior College head football coach Lyle Smith, a true local legend and incredibly nice man still wonders more than four decades later how a coach with his "conservative" philosophy ever hired Tony Knap and his revolutionary ideas about offensive football. Jerry Jackson gave me a history lesson in Idaho high school and college football and more stories than I could print about his famous brother Larry.

Finally, the biggest stars of the show are the many former players who were patient and willing to go into overtime to give candid feedback. All of them were articulate, thoughtful and insightful with their responses.

Time and space did not allow for the inclusion of several players who are all-time greats and significant contributors to the program's success over the years. Lyle Smith doesn't hesitate when asked who the best player he ever coached was. Offensive guard/defensive end Dave Wilcox played two years at Boise Junior College ('60, '61) for Smith before moving on to the University of Oregon, where he was an All-American. An outstanding eleven-year career as a linebacker in the NFL earned him a Hall of Fame berth in 2000.

Five former players who must also be recognized are quarterback Joe Aliotti, defensive tackle Randy Trautman, safety Rick Woods, running back David Hughes and defensive lineman John Rade. The first four were members of the 1980 Division IAA national championship team, while Rade transferred from Modesto Junior College and played for the Broncos in the '81 and '82 seasons. Aliotti was the D-IAA first team *Associated Press* All-American quarterback in '79; Troutman was a two-time first team All-American and the only Bronco player to be inducted into the College Football Hall of Fame. Woods was a second team All-American in '81, and both he and Hughes went on to six-year NFL careers. Trautman and Woods were local Treasure Valley products. Rade went on to a nine-year NFL career that included eight years as a starting linebacker for the Atlanta Falcons.

TABLE OF CONTENTS

Foreword 15
Introduction 19
The Fiesta of All Fiestas 25
Mid-Major vs. Major 37
What's in a Rating? 47
Blue Chip 57
Number One 71
Who are These Guys? 81
In the Beginning. 89
Magic of "The Blue" 103
Football in the Gem State 111
A Dynasty in the Making. 121
Overachievers or Overlooked? 131
Talent is as Talent Does 141
What's the Formula? 155
A Philosophy for Winning. 167
They're no Boise State 183
What a Great Place to Live 197

FOREWORD

Running onto Honolulu, Hawaii's, Aloha Stadium field as a twenty-year-old redshirt freshman in the fall of 1999, I faced my first true test as a Division I defensive lineman. At 5 foot 10, 270 pounds, I was well under the physical dimensions expected for a player at my position. But, then again, so were most of the guys I played with. Outfitted in my patchwork Russell Athletic jersey, and three-year-old well-worn turf shoes, little did I know that my time at Boise State would be the foundation for a winning consistency that would be unmatched by any other D-I university over the next ten years.

The experts wonder why, in a relatively short time, Boise State has been able to achieve so much with so little. Undersized players, lackluster facilities, half the budget of its contemporaries and three different head coaches in ten years wouldn't seem to be a formula for great success. The short answer: an unwavering, unalterable commitment. Everything else is fluff and immaterial.

Every organization seeks leaders who can elicit commitment from his/her subordinates, but finding and maintaining people with these skills is difficult. In my five years at Boise State, I played for two head coaches and one assistant who would eventually become head coach that I consider to be the finest leaders I have ever been associated with. Each brought his own style and left his own footprint on the program, but one thread of consistency that ran through all three was a demand for commitment from every individual who was part of the team.

Each head coach was supremely knowledgeable with regards to his understanding of the game and how to teach, train, and organize young men such that they could win football games. But, just as important, they all recognized the right recruit fit for the program. Sure, every coach wants 6 foot 6 and 300 pounds, but sometimes a tack hammer works better than a sledge hammer. They proved that 5 foot 10 and committed could often out produce 6 foot 3 and suspect.

During my time at Boise State, every player knew on paper he was more often than not undersized, outgunned, and overmatched. But for all the quantifiable figures, the forty-yard run times, the prep-star ratings, and the multi-million dollar budgets, each and every Bronco knew that no one worked harder: player-run off-season practices and drills, 100 percent attendance for "voluntary" summer workouts, 5:45 a.m. workouts in the dead of winter, countless hours of film. We believed in each other, we held each other accountable, we believed no one could beat us. Most of the time, the guys on the other side of the field didn't believe they could beat us either.

In *Blue Collar Mentality*, Tom Barbour examines the unparalleled success Boise State University has achieved without the advantages of rosters stocked with blue chip athletes or decades of storied tradition. Boise State's rise to national prominence, punctuated by its unforgettable victory over Oklahoma in the 2007 Tostitos' Fiesta Bowl, is a story Hollywood couldn't write. Tom deftly navigates the course of Bronco football to find what makes a program built on the backs of try-out walk-ons, grayshirts, and 2-star "'tweeners," so special.

Go Orange, Go Big Blue

Fight, Fight B-S-U!

—Tony Altieri
Boise State
Defensive Tackle '99- '02

INTRODUCTION

A contrarian, in the vernacular of the investment world, is one who seeks to buy stocks that are often out of favor in the eyes of most investors. In 1996, when Boise State University joined the ranks of Division IA, only the most optimistic contrarian would have envisioned the almost overnight transformation of the Broncos into a mid-major college football dynasty.

With little notoriety outside of a blue playing surface, a twelve-year span in the eighties and nineties that produced only moderate returns compared to its principal conference rivals, austere facilities and player values below the average of the market, Boise

State football appeared relegated to several years of major construction before the program might enjoy even a modicum of success.

Fast forward to January 1, 2007. When Boise State rushed onto the University of Phoenix Stadium football field in Glendale, Arizona for the New Year's Day Fiesta Bowl game to take on the University of Oklahoma, the Broncos had already soared well beyond nearly everyone's wildest expectations before the game even began.

A Southern California sports radio talk show host told his audience before the game that Boise State was in a position to begin a new tradition, or be party to a very old one. The old one held by the Sooners covered 111 years, seven consensus national championships since 1950, five Heisman Trophy winners, three College Football Hall of Fame coaches, major college football's best winning percentage since World War II and America's highest paid college coach Bob Stoops.

Boise State counted thirty-five years of junior college play, ten in Division II, eighteen years as a Division IAA participant and eleven years in D-IA. In seventy-four years of fielding football teams the Broncos won a NJCAA Championship in 1958 and the D-IAA Championship in 1980.

As a new member of the Big West Conference a decade earlier, the Broncos were the only conference member not to enjoy a tradition of four-year football dating back to before or shortly after the turn of the twentieth century. Boise State began as Boise Junior College in 1932, didn't officially begin playing football until 1933, and nearly closed its doors due to low enrollment during World War II. The school finally gained four-year standing in 1965, but not until three years later did Boise State field its first four-year team.

When Boise State entered the Western Athletic Conference in 2001, the tradition gap between the Broncos and other conference members seemed to widen. Every WAC university preceded BSU to Division I, some by more than fifty years, and all could rely on much larger alumni bases and major college recruiting pipelines built up by years of networking.

In its initial season of WAC membership, Boise State was celebrating only five years as a Division I participant, yet the program was breaking in its fourth head coach since 1996. Just four years later at the end of the 2005 season, there would be another exchange of coaches.

The student body, campus infrastructure and financial foundation for Boise State also stray from the tradition maintained by most of the other conference members. The student population is dominated by off-campus commuters who comprise 92 percent of the student body, and BSU's endowment fund ranks seventh of the nine conference members, placing it among the lowest of all Football Bowl Subdivision universities.

If major variances in football tradition compared to conference associates wasn't enough, the Broncos carried the stigma of being labeled the second best college football team in the state of Idaho. From 1982 through 1998 the University of Idaho owned the annual rivalry game generating a 15–2 record that included a twelve-game winning streak.

With few if any obvious advantages, quite remarkably, Boise State would rise up to produce the Big West Conference's final two champions before football was phased out at the end of 2000, and in its first season of play, emerge as one of the Western Athletic Conference's preeminent teams, eventually ending the 2001 campaign as conference co-runner-up. From the second season through 2008, the Broncos have dominated the WAC to the extent that only two conference members, Fresno State and Hawaii, own one win each over Boise State.

Conference teams are not the only victims of the Bronco juggernaut: Boise State owns the best winning percentage in all of major college football since 1998 and through the eleven-year period ending in the 2008 season.

The Broncos' stunning upset of Oklahoma in the Fiesta Bowl was not the beginning of a football dynasty, nor was it likely the culmination of one. The victory demonstrated that a program previously considered by many in the national college football media to be of the plucky variety, but not a serious challenge to the BCS establishment, must possess some kind of tradition even if it isn't the Sooners' version.

Between 2,500 and 3,000 high school and junior college players sign letters of intent to receive a scholarship and play football at one of the 120 FBS universities each year. Only about 1 percent of those will choose Boise State. Assembling a group of players each season to form a competitive major college football team is one thing. Creating a series of teams that have won 82 percent of their games over an eleven-year span is another.

This book is not a technical manual with an exhaustive analysis of football theory or Xs and Os. What it does offer is some insight into Boise State's unusual ability to consistently "outperform the market" by a wide margin, with players that are no better than the average of all the players in its principal market. Since it is past and current players, coaches and administrators who have given the Bronco football program its identity, and yes tradition, they all deserve to be examined much more closely. It is the synergy created by this ever-evolving group of people that places Boise State in a class where it "doesn't take long to call roll."

THE FIESTA OF ALL FIESTAS

By today's standards for scholarship athletes this was one of the more unconventional assortment of players to stock a major college football team—the heavy-smoking high school defensive back/wide receiver who sold marijuana to his friends, a prep all-state baseball and basketball star who only played quarterback on the football team to pass the time during the fall months, and the former non-scholarship, walk-on defensive tackle who was so lightly regarded that he was forced to sell his way into a tryout. These were only a few of the mostly low-rated and/or overlooked high school prospects that formed the core of leaders who would take on one of the monsters of college football, the University of Oklahoma, in a major New Year's Day bowl game.

The Boise State University Broncos seemed out of place, if not overmatched, as they ran onto the University of Phoenix Stadium playing field in Glendale, Arizona, for the Bowl Championship Series Fiesta Bowl on January 1, 2007. By virtue of a softening of the selection rules and the addition of a fifth BCS sanctioned bowl game, the undefeated Broncos were recipients of what might be termed by many as a "free pass" to one of the marquee bowls. Additionally, a segment of the college football media establishment felt that the team from the Western Athletic Conference did not represent the quality opponent one would expect for a top-five, postseason bowl contest.

Admittedly, the Broncos boasted an unblemished 12–0 record, but victories over conference members Fresno State, Hawaii, and Nevada did not seem to match Oklahoma's triumphs over Nebraska, Missouri, and Texas Tech in the Big 12.

Many of the Boise State players would admit later that they were apprehensive about the matchup prior to boarding their charter flight for the Phoenix, Arizona, metro area a week before the game. However, after several days of intense, game-style physical contact, almost to a man the players were convinced that they were superior to their Big 12 champion counterparts.

Circus

As the Fiesta Bowl sellout crowd, equally balanced with Bronco and Sooner supporters, greeted their respective teams for the start of the game, Fox Sports television commentator Thom Brennaman brought the contest into perspective when he asked, "Can the little dog play with the big dog?" That question was answered quickly enough when Boise State jumped out to a 14–0 lead after only seven and a half minutes of play. A solid defense that forced two turnovers and contained one of the top rushing offenses in the Big 12, along with an offense that kept the Big 12's best defense off balance, allowed the Broncos to take a 21–10 lead to the locker room at halftime.

Many observers expected Oklahoma to insert halftime adjustments that would overwhelm the pesky Broncos in the third quarter. Instead, a stalemate of sorts ensued, with both defenses stiffening. Then, Boise State capitalized on two more Sooner turnovers. The first, a pass interception by Bronco safety Gerald Alexander, halted an Oklahoma drive but did not end with a Boise State score. On Oklahoma's next possession, after a BSU punt, Sooner quarterback Paul Thompson threw a first-down pass from his own twenty-four yard line that was tipped at the line of scrimmage and intercepted by Bronco safety Marty Tadman, who scampered twenty-seven yards to the end zone, giving BSU a 28–10 lead.

The Broncos appeared to take command of the game when the defense ended a Sooner six-play drive on their next possession at the BSU forty-six yard line, forcing a fourth-down punt. With five and a half minutes left in the third quarter, delirious Boise State fans were starting to believe the unbelievable—if they had dominated the Sooners for almost three quarters, it seemed reasonable to assume that the Broncos could maintain that edge for the final one. What the boisterous crowd, now joined by a growing television audience who had tuned in to watch the upset in the making, didn't know was that the first three quarters were only a warm-up band before the headliner.

Bronco Nation could hardly believe what transpired in the fourth quarter of play. The turnover bug that had plagued the Sooners in the first three quarters bit the Broncos at the end of the third and again in the fourth. A comfortable eighteen-point lead was suddenly a tie game after Oklahoma quarterback Paul Thompson's touchdown pass to wide receiver Quentin Chaney and two-point conversion toss with just one minute and fifteen seconds to play.

On the initial play of BSU's first possession after the kick-off, Oklahoma cornerback Marcus Walker intercepted quarterback Jared Zabransky's poorly executed pass and returned it thirty-four yards for a touchdown to put the Sooners up by seven, leaving only sixty-two seconds for a Bronco comeback attempt. Suddenly depressed Bronco fans were confronted with the possibility they had just witnessed a third consecutive season-ending bowl loss due to a Zabransky interception.

On the first play following the kick-off, Boise State showing some spark with a clutch thirty-six-yard pass from Zabransky to tight end Derek Schouman, spotting the ball on the Sooner forty-two; the adrenaline started to flow again. But after a quarterback sack, two incomplete passes, and eight yards of losses, reality began to set in that the previous thirty-second interval, in what seemed like an eternity, had only been a cruel delay of the inevitable. The Broncos were now faced with a fourth and eighteen for a first down, fifty yards from a touchdown, with only eighteen seconds on the game clock. What happened next is magical beyond words to Bronco fans.

With the deep lanes and sidelines covered by extra defensive backs, Zabransky aimed what appeared to be an ill-advised fifteen-yard pass to receiver Drisan James, who had run a crossing pattern from the left side to the dead center of the field and right into the middle of pass coverage. As James caught the pass and his momentum was about to carry him into the arms and shoulders of three defenders, he turned and pitched the ball back to wide receiver Jerard Rabb, who was darting across the field from the opposite direction. With all of the defenders converging on James, Rabb sprinted thirty-five yards to the end zone for the score. The hook-and-lateral play identified as "Circus" would prolong to overtime what many pundits called the most exciting college football game ever played.

Statue

Boise State was now on its eighth play of overtime with a fourth and two at the Oklahoma five yard line, attempting to match the Sooners' one-play, twenty-five yard touchdown run by star running back Adrian Peterson. On the sidelines, due to an official's timeout to review the previous play, head coach Chris Petersen and quarterback Zabransky were in total disagreement about what to do next. Petersen and offensive coordinator Brian Harsin had decided to call a play that would put the ball, and the Broncos' fate, in the hands of a former walk-on, sophomore utility player Vinny Perretta, with a direct snap pass/run option.

Fifth-year senior Zabransky, overseer of thirty-two victories in three years, was decidedly and maybe justifiably agitated. If anyone should be allowed to win or lose the biggest game in Boise State history, it was him. Though Z produced team offensive MVP performances in bowl games against Louisville and Boston College, both were heartbreaking losses, in which he threw a game ending interception in one and a rally ending interception with thirty-seven seconds left in the other.

The coaches won the brief sideline dispute during the timeout, and so Zabransky, instead of touching the ball, would line up as a running back and act as a decoy, shifting in motion the opposite direction of the play. Perretta took a direct snap from center in the shotgun, tucked the ball, and looked to sweep right. Tight end Derek Schouman who lined up as a wide receiver on the right side feigned a shoulder block on outside linebacker Rufus Alexander, and then angled for the right corner of the end zone. The inside linebacker, Zach Latimer, immediately picked up Schouman and ran with him step for step. Perretta pulled up from his running position and calmly lofted a perfect lob pass over Latimer into the outstretched hands of Schouman for the touchdown.

With the drama already at a fever pitch, the Boise State coaching staff cranked it to a little higher crescendo when they left place kicker Anthony Montgomery on the bench and showed a two-point conversion attempt to win rather than tie the game. One of the Fox Network game crew, Charles Davis, had already anticipated the Bronco decision and announced it almost immediately after the touchdown. He sensed, as did many watching, that the Boise State players were emotionally and physically spent and would be hard-pressed to withstand another offensive barrage from the Sooners. Oklahoma coach Bob Stoops immediately called a timeout to converse with his players and coaches about what the Broncos might pull next from their bag of trick plays.

BSU head coach Chris Petersen would admit during a postgame interview that his backup quarterbacks convinced him to run the next play. Unlike the hook-and-lateral play, which had never been executed in a game situation, "Statue" had fared well at a critical juncture in an earlier regular season game against the University of Idaho. With all the wide receivers split to the right side, Zabransky under center, and star running back Ian Johnson behind him, the quarterback took the snap and faked a throw with an empty right hand as he slipped the ball behind his back with his left. With nearly all of the defense's reaction to the Broncos' right side, Johnson took the ball from his quarterback and sprinted untouched to the left corner of the end zone.

An Inauspicious Start

When the football program embarked on its Division I journey in 1996, Boise State found itself in a moderate-success syndrome. From 1982 through 1993, the Broncos could produce no better than a single runner-up finish and a total of four post season playoff games in the Big Sky Conference. The University of Idaho with fifteen post season games, and the University of Nevada Reno with fourteen, dominated the conference, between them winning or sharing nine of twelve Big Sky Conference crowns. It was during that span of twelve seasons that Idaho groomed three head coaches for eventual Division I, major conference (BCS today) team head coaching positions.

In 1994, the Broncos finally scored a win over Idaho after twelve consecutive annual losses, captured a Big Sky title and subsequently played for the D-IAA national championship, which they lost to Youngstown State. BSU came down quickly from its mountaintop experience of '94 to post a pedestrian 7–4 record and resumption of a new losing streak against Idaho in 1995. Though the program owned a winning record, Boise State possessed little in the way of sustained high-level performance over the previous fourteen seasons to distinguish itself from new Big West Conference partners Idaho and Nevada.

After a slow start and only two wins in the new conference, followed by four and six wins respectively for '97 and '98, there was still not much substance to the Bronco football program in the recruiting season of 1999 to compel high school or junior college players to choose Boise State if they were presented with alternatives to play elsewhere. Nevada, after departing the Big Sky to enter the Big West Conference in '92, overwhelmed Boise State with three consecutive blowout victories from '96 through '98 and Idaho won a conference championship along with two of its three regular season matchups against the Broncos (Nevada was the Big West champion or co-champion for five of its first six years in the conference).

Two consecutive Big West titles in '99 and '00 for Boise State was definitely a positive trend, but could hardly be considered a panacea for attracting blue chip recruits when the conference shut down football after the 2000 season and the Broncos were obliged to move to a new one.

Transitioning from the Big West to the Western Athletic Conference produced similar recruiting angst to that so painfully experienced by the coaches in the move from D-IAA to D-IA. The WAC presented a whole new set of teams (Nevada left the Big West and joined the WAC in 2000) all with considerably more recruiting clout and tradition than Boise State.

Braveheart

As a young preteen, Bart Hendricks rushed the field in 1990 after the number one ranked University of Nevada, Reno, football team edged Boise State in a thrilling overtime Division IAA semi-final playoff game. Hendricks went on to play football in high school, but Procter R. Hug High in Reno only won three games during his senior year.

If there was ever a quarterback prospect a head coach should recruit to lead his college football program to the next level, it did not appear to be Bart Hendricks. Hendricks was a scrapper, but his overall skills and size were not at the level most Division I programs were seeking.

Though he had been a big University of Nevada football fan growing up, he received only lukewarm attention from the Wolf Pack coaching staff in the fall of 1995 after his senior season and was expected to walk-on. Boise State head coach, Pokey Allen, who recognized qualities that may not have seemed apparent to other Division I coaches, sent assistants to Reno to offer Hendricks a scholarship. The Nevada coaches had second thoughts and also tendered a scholarship, but Hendricks had already made his decision to become a Bronco.

After two years as a starter/backup, Hendricks earned mixed reviews for his overall performance. A sportswriter for the local *Idaho Statesman* newspaper seemed to have made up his mind, however, when he announced that one thing was certain: Bart Hendricks would never lead Boise State to a conference championship.

With his heart, legs and arm, Hendricks turned his detractors on their heads when he engineered BSU's first Big West Conference championship teams and first Division I Bowl wins, established ten new Bronco quarterback records (including the leader in single season touchdown passes—a BSU record he held through the 2008 season), and was voted Big West Conference Player of the Year twice.

In 2000, his last college season, Hendricks garnered the number one efficiency rating in all of Division I with a 170.6, compared to the top three vote-getters for the Heisman Trophy: Chris Weinke, Florida State (163.1); Josh Heupel, Oklahoma (139.2); and Drew Brees, Purdue (132.4). He capped off his career with an MVP performance in the 2000 Humanitarian Bowl that included a seventy-seven yard run for a touchdown, two touchdown passes, and a twelve-yard touchdown catch!

During his junior and senior years, BSU had a win/loss record of 20-5 while the team that all but spurned him, University of Nevada, was 5-18. In 1999, when Hendricks led the Broncos to a 52-17 rout of Nevada, the Wolf Pack coaches may have started second guessing themselves about their opportunity to be the first to offer him a scholarship four years earlier.

MID-MAJOR VS. MAJOR

NCAA Division I or D-I (officially Division IA beginning in 1978) is a common reference to "major" college football conferences and teams. The official designation (since 2004) for the current group of 120 Division I schools is Football Bowl Subdivision (FBS). The FBS is divided into Bowl Championship Series (BCS) conferences (six), and non-BCS conferences (five) and three independents (Notre Dame, Army and Navy). For the most part, BCS conference teams are the more traditional long-standing college football programs, whereas most of the non-BCS teams are smaller, less-established programs. All FBS members are identified as "major" college football programs, while non-BCS conference members are sometimes referred to as "mid-majors". The balance of colleges operating football programs play in one of four additional divisions: Football Championship Subdivision (FCS), previously referred to as Division IAA; Division II; Division III; and National Association of Interscholastic Athletics (NAIA).

Alexander's Rag Tag Band

By the fall of 2001, cousins Gerald and Rufus Alexander had each reached his senior year in high school. Gerald was on the honor roll at Southern California's Rancho Cucamonga High School and a dual sport athlete, excelling in track as a high jumper and football as a quarterback. He was good enough as a football player to be his league's MVP, along with selection to a regional all-star team. Rufus, having been rescued from abject poverty by surrogate parents David and Linda Barham in the small southern Louisiana town of Breaux Bridge, was considered by several recruiting information services to be one of the top outside linebacker prospects in the country.

As national letter of intent day approached on the first Wednesday of February, 2002, a time when high school football players commit to specific colleges to accept scholarships, coaches all but camped on the front lawn of the Barhams's home. Several major college programs in the Midwest and Southeast were working overtime to woo the 6 foot 1, 215 pound linebacker. On the West Coast, in Southern California, football scholarship prospects for Gerald were limited. Though he had been a versatile athlete and an excellent high school quarterback, at six foot, 170 pounds, he was considered by college recruiters to be on the small side, possessing only average arm strength and running speed.

While Rufus was sifting through mail and phone messages, trying to decide which of the many scholarship offers to accept, Gerald didn't need to sift at all. He received only two. On commitment day, Rufus signed his letter of intent to play at a university with a long history of multiple conference and national championships, a school many consider to have consistently been one of the best college football programs in America for the last sixty years. Gerald signed with a relatively small mid-major university that had only been playing NCAA Division I football for six years. The program, at least on the surface, appeared to be in flux, breaking in the fifth head coach in seven years and forced in the prior year to join a new conference when the previous one eliminated football.

Fast-forward five years to the late fall of 2006, as both players were finishing their fifth-year senior seasons. Rufus was closing out a stellar career as a linebacker that included being selected to three All-American teams and named the Big-12 Conference Defensive Player of the Year as a senior. When he made solo tackles at home games, 84,000 partisan fans rose in unison, calling out "Ruuuufus." By contrast, Gerald enjoyed a solid career, was able to make the starting lineup at cornerback and later as a safety, but never earned even postseason honorable mention to his conference all-star team.

Though these players received contrasting individual recognition over their careers, the respective college football teams they played for were surprisingly close in terms of their success. It was not unexpected that Rufus' team compiled a five-year record of 54–11, played in five consecutive bowl games, won three conference championships, and enjoyed national rankings every year between number three and number twenty-two. During the same five-year period, Gerald's team came from near obscurity to post an even better record (56–7), won its conference every year with only one conference loss, was victorious in every regular season home game, went to five consecutive bowl games, and was nationally ranked at the end of the seasons for four of the five years between number five and number sixteen.

The Bowl Championship Series (BCS) was devised in 1998 by the six largest conferences for major college football, in order to theoretically better determine the national champion. This is facilitated through a computer-generated, universal ranking system that ultimately places the number one and number two ranked teams in a championship game at the end of the bowl season. In addition to the national championship game, the BCS also designates four additional major bowl games as part of the BCS package. Thanks to the insertion of rule changes for the 2006 season, allowing non-BCS conference teams a greater chance to be named to one of the BCS bowl games, Gerald's team was awarded a major bowl appearance. For only the second time in the BCS system's nine-year history, a lesser established, mid-major school (University of Utah was the first in 2005) was named to play in a BCS bowl game.

On January 1, 2007, in prime time, a national television audience watched underdog but undefeated Boise State University, with its first-year head coach Chris Petersen and only eleven seasons of Division I history, square off against favored giant of college football University of Oklahoma in the Fiesta Bowl. Rufus Alexander was deservedly the focus of the Fox telecast team's pregame chatter due to his outstanding career. Gerald Alexander, the unheralded safety for the Broncos, was not even announced as the star of his own defensive backfield; that distinction went to junior Marty Tadman.

Rufus, who would meet his cousin for the first time during the week prior to the bowl game, left no doubt about his abilities when he made seventeen tackles and proved to be the outstanding defensive player for his team. On the other side, Gerald played in only his thirteenth game at safety. He was proving, however, that the move from cornerback, his position for the first three years, to safety, was one that showcased strengths not so evident while playing his previous position.

Boise State's electrifying 43–42 overtime victory, making them the only undefeated team in the FBS for 2006–2007, was given every superlative imaginable by the pundits, including being called the most exciting college football game ever played. If the Broncos were the quintessential underdog, then cousins Gerald and Rufus Alexander represented a microcosm of their respective teams. By virtue of his outstanding college career, Rufus was being touted as at least a first-day pick in the upcoming draft and knew he would be invited to the NFL Scouting Combine, where elite college players are tested for speed, strength, and agility. Gerald, on the other hand, had no illusions that a guaranteed invitation was imminent. He could only wait and hope that NFL scouts might have seen something in his senior year that would entice them to put him on the list.

Gerald Alexander was a capable, if unspectacular, cornerback for his first three years. Though he worked hard, and with assistance from a young, eager coaching staff improved his technique and increased his speed, he was never truly comfortable at the cornerback position. His defense against the run was superb, and he regularly made hard, sure tackles, but his pass coverage was inconsistent, and he often found himself out of position. The newly named defensive coordinator for Boise State, twenty-nine-year-old Justin Wilcox, agreed to a 2006 spring practice call by the defensive backs' coach Marcel Yates to move Alexander to safety. With the weight-room sculpted thirty-five pounds he added to the 170 since high school, and a penchant for making big plays and bone-jarring tackles, it was obvious to the coaches and other players by the final spring scrimmage that he had found the position he probably should have been playing all along.

In the fall of 2006, Gerald's first four games as a safety were routine, and though he did not have overwhelming statistics, the coaches were delighted with the way he "kept all of the action in front of him." In the fifth game, against the University of Utah, he seemed to come out of his shell. He showed great athleticism with an interception, and on another play, he knifed through blockers to hit Utah running back Darryl Poston so hard that he knocked the player's helmet off.

He was only tenth out of the eleven starting defensive players in total tackles for the regular season, but it was clear to many before the Fiesta Bowl that he had very quickly acquired the skills to play his new position. In the bowl game he shone again, leaping high to intercept a pass and return it twenty-five yards. But it was his one-on-one tackle of Oklahoma's All-American and future NFL star, Adrian Peterson, near the goal line that demonstrated what Gerald Alexander was capable of doing. With speed, agility, and strength, he read the running play perfectly and ran the swift Peterson down behind the line of scrimmage with a take-down solo tackle.

Gerald did receive an invitation to the Scouting Combine, along with his much more famous relative, Rufus. Combine experts viewed Gerald as a solid performer at the seven-day event, with a respectable 4.5 second forty-yard run, and finishing near the top of the other agility drills. His vertical jump of forty-one inches was second best of all 327 players. Rufus, on the other hand, was not posting good numbers. All of his measurables were well below the standards that were expected for high draft choices at linebacker. Because he had been such a great college player with exceptional career statistics, many scouts were taken by surprise.

When draft weekend arrived, Gerald hoped to be selected by the end of the second day but also knew that there was a chance he might not be drafted at all. To almost everyone's surprise, the Detroit Lions made two trades to move up several draft positions and take Gerald in the second round as the sixty-first player overall. Rufus waited until the sixth round and was the 176th player selected, taken by Minnesota. Gerald had never been so much as an honorable mention pick in what many football experts consider a low-grade conference. The NFL scouts, however, saw things a bit differently when only two of seventeen total Western Athletic Conference players drafted, both from the University of Hawaii, were selected ahead of him, in positions fifty-eight and sixty of the second round.

None of the major recruiting information services included Gerald Alexander in their lists of nationally ranked high school defensive back prospects in 2002. In the same year, nearly one hundred high school football players from Southern California, where Alexander lived, accepted scholarships to play on BCS-member Pacific-10 Conference teams, though none of those ten schools ever made an offer to Alexander. On April 28, 2007, Gerald said he was doing his laundry when a phone call came from the NFL with the message that he was a second round draft pick. Only five safeties were chosen ahead of him, but each was an All-American and an expected high draft choice.

Sudden Impact

Korey Hall is the stereotypical, "they grow 'em big and strong out in the country" young man who was raised in the potato-growing high plains of south central Idaho. He attended a small school in Glenns Ferry, along a bend in the winding Snake River, and is a legend as a high school player. If you ask folks in Glenns Ferry and surrounding towns about Hall, they claim in glowing terms that he is the best football player they ever saw. He terrorized Southern Idaho Division 2-A opponents for four years as a linebacker and running back. Surprisingly, after his senior season, the 2001 2-A all-state player of the year didn't receive a Division I scholarship offer from a school other than Boise State. It appears recruiters rationalized that he lacked the minimum size/speed numbers.

Middle linebacker Hall was not the announced defensive player of the game in the 2007 Fiesta Bowl, for that honor went to junior safety, Marty Tadman, who happened to snatch a couple of key interceptions. After the game, Tadman thanked Hall for tipping the ball at the line of scrimmage, allowing him the extra time he needed to anticipate the ball's trajectory and make his second interception. During several defensive stands in the first half, former Wisconsin head coach, Barry Alvarez, the excellent color commentator for the Fox Sports Network, called Hall's name on what seemed like every play. Tadman played extremely well, but for most who watched with a critical eye, Korey Hall was equally deserving of the official title as defensive player of the game.

Hall finished his college career as a *Sporting News* All-American, three-time first-team all-conference middle linebacker, and WAC defensive player of the year in 2006. He produced so many outstanding plays in the Fiesta Bowl that the game could easily have substituted for his own personal highlight video. When his college career ended, almost everyone who had watched Bronco football since 1968 agreed there was no better player to don the orange and blue than Korey Hall.

While most NFL draft experts admitted he was truly a great college player, they assessed his skills to be below the minimum requirements for success at the next level. Hall didn't surprise Bronco fans when he went on to become the starting fullback and special teams ace for the Green Bay Packers in his rookie year of 2007.

WHAT'S IN A RATING?

When Jared Zabransky and Ian Johnson combined to run the play called "Statue" to win the Fiesta Bowl, some key components of the deception in the play were the actions taken by left tackle Ryan Clady. Clady needed to appear as if he were pass blocking in order to entice the defensive end to make his move toward the quarterback, then within a split second pull out to the edge and position himself to help block any defensive player who read the play. He did his job perfectly and the rest is history.

Clady was a quiet, laid back, 6 foot 6, 317 pound giant of a young man from Rialto, California, who attended Eisenhower High School, the alma mater of USC great and NFL Hall of Famer Ronnie Lott. A once proud and powerful football program, Eisenhower has fallen on hard times in recent years, and Clady played on poor teams. In high school, Clady was mostly positioned on the defensive line and chose not to attend any college camps, so by the end of his senior year he was very much an unknown. He was given a non-blue chip two-star rating by the major recruit information services and only two or three mid-major programs recruited him. Boise State head coach Dan Hawkins envisioned Clady as an offensive lineman and was the first to offer a firm scholarship.

Underneath his quiet demeanor the wheels started churning in spring practice after his redshirt season. It was obvious to coaches after his freshman year that Clady had a combination of athletic ability and size never seen before in an offensive lineman at Boise State. At the beginning of his sophomore year he slipped into the left tackle position vacated by the seemingly irreplaceable 2006 second round draft pick, Daryn Colledge, and dominated almost from the beginning. By the end of his junior year, with one more year of eligibility, Clady was a consensus All-American and all but a guaranteed first round draft choice.

Wasting little time, Clady quickly declared himself eligible for the 2008 draft. Within a matter of days from his declaration, Clady's name went to the top of the draft board. On April 26, he was the twelfth player selected and became the first number one draft pick in BSU history. Clady became an opening day starter at the key left tackle position for the Denver Broncos, and by the end of the '08 season was named second team All-Pro and considered by knowledgeable NFL analysts to be one of the top offensive linemen in the league.

Pick your Prospects

As the college football season begins to wind down to its inevitable conclusion each fall, serious fans and alumni, especially those not preoccupied by visions of a new coach for an underachieving program, begin the process of critiquing the list of new recruits for the upcoming year. Prospect watching has always been good sport, but beginning in the early 2000s, the pastime exploded into what has become a multi-million dollar business with the proliferation of dozens of recruiting information websites.

Sites like *Rivals.com* and *Scout.com* monitor and dole out data on prospects from Miami, Florida to Hilo, Hawaii. For a monthly or annual subscription fee, one can follow the recruiting process of his/her college team compared to all teams by reviewing message boards with updates for individual prospects along with videos and press releases on all players in the database.

Recruiting Division I football players can be as much art as science, and almost every head coach has a philosophy on the subject that he will impart if pressed to do so. There is, however, only one unspoken, universal school of thought among head coaches, and it is this: if his football program has comparable facilities, technicians, and motivators to those of his opposing teams, he is likely to generate more wins than losses in a season if his players are superior to those of the other teams. For that reason, the competition for the best players in the land is fierce.

The recruiting information services, through their teams of scouts and contacts, keep tabs on presumably every high school and junior college player qualified for Division I. *Rivals* and *Scout* use a system that rates a prospect in several key categories, and then assigns him a number from one to five stars, with five as the highest. Five-star ratings are reserved for only about the top thirty to thirty-five elite players in the country each year. On the other end of the spectrum, one-star ratings are generally given to players judged as marginal or below Division I quality. Two-star prospects are the largest category, leaving three- and four-stars as the majority of what are termed "blue chips." Coaches, like poker players, want the equivalent of a full house on the field when they open up a new season, so blue chip players are in great demand.

With the exception of a few—those sometimes affectionately referred to as freaks—for players with physical characteristics placing them in an elite size/strength/power/speed range category, rating can be somewhat arbitrary. The basic criteria for judging the value of a prospect boil down to game performance, measurables (size/speed/quickness/strength), and what coaches and analysts refer to as intangibles.

Only recently, the rating gurus have developed something called the SPARQ, an acronym for Speed, Power, Agility, Reaction, and Quickness. SPARQ is a formula that combines, among other drills, the forty-yard dash, twenty-yard shuttle run, bench press, and vertical jump into a single number to measure overall athleticism. The numbers speak for themselves, but the intangibles, such as character, leadership qualities, work ethic, position presence/awareness, heart, and drive, are much more subjective.

In simplest terms, with assumed similar game performance and intangibles, a running back at 6 foot, 205 pounds with a 4.45 time in the forty-yard run and a bench press of 300 pounds, will usually receive a higher rating than one at, 5 foot 9, 180 pounds, 4.6 forty and a 280 pounds bench press. Different positions, of course, create emphasis on different measurables. For example, height and speed are most important for receivers, height, arm strength and throwing accuracy for quarterbacks, and height, weight, strength, and power for linemen.

The established major football programs have long had a monopoly on the highest rated players. With tradition and huge networks of alumni on their side, they are, for the most part, guaranteed a quota of blue chips by simply making scholarship offers to their target market of best prospects. In the 2008 recruiting class, for example, according to *Rivals.com*, only one of the top 250 high school prospects across the country picked a non-BCS conference school to attend.

In many cases, the biggest challenge for top programs is determining a means to out-maneuver their rivals for a share in the thirty to thirty-five elite players available each year. Just two or three five-star prospects added to a team's mix could make the difference between a twelve-win and ten-win season down the road.

Most of the upper tier BCS teams evaluate the nucleus of blue chip players they want to pursue by the end of their junior year of high school. This allows them to focus resources and attention on these players well before mid-major and lower tier major programs. As a result, the elite schools are usually able to elicit a verbal commitment from most of their best prospects before their senior year in high school, several months in advance of the February letter of intent signing date. Mid-major programs are often forced to wait and see if players may develop into D-I prospects during their senior year and/or are left over after the major programs have picked their scholarship recruits.

Most mid-majors do not have the notoriety, tradition, media exposure, and budgets of the major programs, so they must be much more creative in their recruiting techniques and player development. Major football programs are able to acquire more highly skilled and well-developed players who are, in many instances, ready to play in their true freshman season. In the Pac-10, for example, by mid-season 2008, seventy-nine true freshmen had played in a game.

Major schools will often place strict minimum measurable standards on most positions for which they are willing to offer scholarships. Mid-majors have found that they can loosen the requirements and find very capable players. A 5 foot 11, 195 pound high school linebacker may not receive a second look from many major programs for the same position in college, but if he has the speed, athleticism and/or intangibles of a player two to three inches taller and twenty pounds heavier, he might be a first-line recruit for a mid-major.

Many high school players start playing football later than their peers, and have yet to develop skills through practice and repetition. Other players may become injured in their important junior or even senior year, when the major programs are evaluating prospects. Coaches from non-BCS programs have become skilled at judging these players (usually with the help of the high school coach) with a short span of observation and evaluation.

To be competitive, mid-majors must always be on the lookout for the hidden gems that often come from smaller, underdeveloped, or losing high school programs. Coaching staffs usually find these prospects through a highly developed network, including current players and high school coaches.

Mid-majors also fare much better when they make offers to recruits from the pool of top junior college players. For the 2009 recruiting season for example, non-BCS teams wooed thirty of the top one hundred JC players to their programs. Most of these prospects are ready to play immediately and fulfill roles as starters, special teams members or key back-ups.

Since mid-majors rarely have the luxury of signing large numbers of highly rated high school prospects with the size and skill to play D-I immediately, or even after a redshirt season, one of the more recent approaches they are taking to develop scholarship players is something called *grayshirting*.

Grayshirting is an unofficial designation for convincing what coaches believe to be a promising but underdeveloped player to sit out with the promise of a scholarship, usually starting the next recruiting cycle. Under NCAA rules, grayshirts are prohibited from practicing or attending team meetings, film sessions, or any other functions during that grayshirt season.

Most players who grayshirt graduate in the spring of their high school senior year (occasionally a prospect will graduate in December/January and grayshirt in the spring semester). In the majority of cases the player sits out the fall term and enrolls in the winter session on scholarship. One of the most attractive features of grayshirting for coaches is that it allows the player to take part in spring practice, but his eligibility clock doesn't start until the next fall. This affords him the opportunity to extend his development time another year with a redshirt season, but adding an extra spring practice not available to immediate scholarship players.

Grayshirting does not preclude a player from beginning an aggressive training regimen during his non-enrolled term. Coaches will encourage the grayshirt to set a schedule on his own that allows him to add football weight and conditioning so that he is prepared for the spring practice session.

There are additional benefits to the team when a prospect agrees to a grayshirt; it immediately frees up another scholarship that may be better-utilized in the current recruiting class by offering it to another more developed player. Grayshirting is rare at the elite major level, since most of these schools are able to acquire a quota of highly skilled players who need much less development by comparison.

Walking Tall

Daryn Colledge was a tall, slender, two-way player from North Pole High School in tiny North Pole, Alaska, pop. 1,700. After his senior year, he was named all-state as an offensive lineman and second team as a defensive lineman. Colledge was not offered a Division I scholarship, but head coach Dan Hawkins convinced him to come to Boise State with the promise of a future scholarship. Hawkins saw great potential in Colledge, but also recognized that if he was going to play on the offensive line in D-I, he needed some added work and time to increase his bulk and strength.

After a semester of delayed full-time enrollment he went on scholarship his next year and participated in spring practice, only to be redshirted in the fall. Colledge became a weight room fanatic, eventually breaking several team lifting records. Though he was raw and still learning the left tackle position, by the beginning of his redshirt freshman year, he had built himself up to a muscular 288 pounds. In BSU's second game of the 2004 season, against Oregon State,

Colledge, now in his junior year, faced arguably the best defensive end in the Pac-10, Bill Swancutt. Colledge didn't just block Swancutt, he dominated him, helping Boise State manhandle OSU and triumph over a Pac-10 team for the first time.

Colledge would end his career with fifty-two consecutive starts, the most of any player in BSU history, three All-WAC selections, an All-American team, and a vote as the number one offensive lineman in the conference his last two years. In the April 2006 NFL draft, he was taken in the second round by Green Bay, forty-seventh overall. In his first year as a member of the Packers he became a starter at left guard, a position he still holds at the beginning of the 2009 season.

BLUE CHIP

Allen Bradford ranked as the top prep football player in the state of California by *Rivals.com* after the 2005 season and considered by many recruiting services as the best defensive player in the country. As an elite five-star player (one of only twenty-eight in the 2006 national high school recruiting class, according to *Rivals*), Bradford received scholarship offers from several top programs, including Oklahoma, but outside of USC, he made official visits to only UCLA, Oregon, and Nebraska.

After playing in the U.S. Army All-American allstar game with other elite high school players from across the nation at the end of the '05 season, he was singled out by several scouts and coaches as the most ferocious hitter and one of the best all around defensive players on either team. When the game ended, he and his best friend and high school teammate, Shareece Wright, a blue chip defensive back, gave verbal commitments to the University of Southern California.

When he began fall practice in 2006, the Trojans were two deep on the roster at each of the linebacker positions, so Bradford accepted head coach Pete Carroll's call to play the safety position.

Bradford dutifully studied the USC defensive schemes for several months after signing his letter of intent, and by mid-preseason practice was asserting himself into a battle for one of the starting safety positions. With only a couple of weeks until the first game and an unusually large number of injuries, especially at the tailback position, coach Carroll asked Bradford if he would move to running back. Carroll told Bradford he saw him as fitting the mold of a LenDale White, USC's former running back who had complemented Heisman Trophy winner Reggie Bush with his power running style only a year earlier.

Bradford's expendability became a reality because USC was well-stocked with safeties in the upper classes and was also blessed with Taylor Mays, one of the best high school safety prospects in the country, another member of USC's 2006 recruiting class. However, USC had so many elite tailbacks that one, Emmanuel Moody, who was pictured on the 2007 cover of the Sports Illustrated Regional College Football edition with fellow running backs C.J. Cable and Chauncey Washington, decided to transfer just a few days before the season even started. At least Moody was recruited as a tailback and knew exactly who and what he was up against; Bradford didn't have that luxury.

It would be understandable if Bradford were disappointed that after three seasons, he has become lost at the bottom of a heap of great running backs, the victim of a program with so many talented players that he was forced to "take a hit" for the betterment of the team. A regional newspaper in the Southern California Inland Empire city of Riverside, near where Bradford attended Colton High School, publicized the fact that he and his father met with Carroll on two occasions to express their puzzlement with his move to offense and lack of playing time. In both hearings, they were promised that "good things were coming."

Though healthy during his freshman and sophomore seasons and three games into the 2008 season before being hobbled by a hip injury, the "good things" that happened to him after three years and thirty games included forty-two rushing attempts for 123 yards, ten pass receptions for one hundred yards, one kick return for nine yards, six touchdowns, and twelve tackles. Though Bradford may very well resurrect his career at USC, these numbers must doubtless be calculated as a personal underachievement so far by a player who generated 1,900 yards rushing, 429 yards receiving, thirty-six touchdowns, 157 tackles, and twelve sacks as a high school senior.

Through the 2008 season, Bradford never started a game for USC, and his role was confined to specific situations on offense and special teams. It's almost a lock that, had he accepted an offer from any of the three schools he visited before signing a letter of intent to play at USC, he would have cracked the starting lineup at linebacker or safety during his freshman year.

The young man who was judged by everyone who saw him play in high school as one of the best defensive players available anywhere hasn't had much of a chance to prove himself. He has demonstrated that he can catch passes and run well enough to score touchdowns at a rate matching his tailback peers, but apparently that's not good enough to warrant considerably more playing time on offense. Instead, he has languished at a position where USC has talent to burn.

Big Difference

A survey of the player rosters for non-California FBS teams in the western states reveals that they are all indebted to the Golden State pipeline of high school and junior college players. Boise State is no exception, counting 44 percent of the listed roster in 2007 from California, while only 16 percent hailed from the home state of Idaho. Even if the players from the six states that border Idaho are included, they only added another 15 percent of all roster players for a total of 31 percent from the region. The lack of home-bred players showed glaringly in the depth chart for Boise State's

2008 season-ending Poinsettia Bowl game, when only seven of fifty-six players were from the state of Idaho.

Though the Broncos made some serious inroads into challenging the Pacific Northwest Pac-10 schools for prospect commitments from Washington and Oregon in 2009, the players choosing Boise State in the past have been at the lower end of the rankings for the region. Boise State must venture to more distant corners of North America like Canada, Texas and even the Eastern Seaboard states of New Jersey, Maryland, Georgia and Florida, where they have found players willing to come to Idaho.

The University of Southern California, by comparison, operates in a different sphere when it comes to recruiting. USC counted three-fourths of its '07 roster from California, and 93 percent of those were from Southern California. The Trojans also travel to the farthest regions of the country, it's simply that the prospects they lure are of much greater value for the travel time and expense.

The stark contrast in recruiting processes and player values for USC and BSU might best be demonstrated in '06 and '07 when both teams received a total forty-three letters of intent from scholarship players. Using the data from *Scout.com,* USC held eighteen five-star players, seventeen four-stars and eight three-stars. Boise State signed one four-star, eleven three-stars, thirty two-stars and one one-star. Boise State drew 81 percent of its recruits from out of state, while USC signed 33 percent of its players from states or Canadian provinces other than California.

Six of the eight players from Idaho for Boise State, in the two recruiting classes, were designated as grayshirts. Five of the six grayshirts were given redshirts in their second season, further extending their development time. All the rest of the '06 recruits were redshirted in their first year, and all but four position players and a kicker in the '07 class received a redshirt (an unusually high number of players for Boise State to advance as true freshmen, when in any previous years only one or two players were typically brought up to play, and often only to replace injured players).

USC's recruit classes of '06 and '07, considered by *Scout.com* to be the number one and number two ranked FBS classes respectively, were not stocked with just your average blue chips; five were classified as the number one player at their respective positions, four at number two, two at number three and four more at number four. Fifteen players from the combined classes advanced to eligibility in their true freshman year, and several, like wide receiver Ronald Johnson and tailbacks Joe McKnight and Stephon Johnson, became key contributors as freshmen.

Boise State's Fiesta Bowl victory has given a great boost to the program's visibility, but did not translate into a flood of blue chip recruits in the 2008 class. According to *Scout*, USC recruited offensive line prospects rated one, three, eight, and ten nationally, while BSU recruited numbers seventy, ninety, 101, and 143. All of USC's offensive line recruits originated in California (three within about a seventy mile radius of the campus), whereas all of BSU's came from out of state, including Texas, Arizona, Washington, and California. Obligated to travel much farther, Boise State was likely required to expend greater resources to recruit lesser-valued players.

At the end of the 2008 college football season, the *Associated Press* final poll ranked a 12–1 USC at number three, and a 12–1 Boise State at number eleven. Not surprisingly, eleven USC players were drafted by NFL teams in 2009, while Boise State was the only member of the top 25 to be without a drafted player.

Barry Every of *Rivals.com* made some interesting observations with respect to the Broncos' recruiting challenges. In a spring 2009 article he stated, "Boise State is the school that has to really hit the recruiting trail hard because Idaho is basically void of D-I talent. I think Boise does a great job of identifying kids who may be a tad short or slow for "Big Six" schools to go after, but these same kids are legit, hard-nosed football players. A good football player with the desire to succeed will beat out a star athlete every time if the star athlete does not find the motivation to get better."

If notoriety, tradition, and media exposure aren't enough to disqualify mid-majors from securing the best of the blue chips, the gargantuan budgets of the majors certainly are. Most of the Southeastern Conference universities own, or lease, private airplanes used almost exclusively to ferry coaches around the country for football and basketball recruiting, and many of the top schools regularly spend $1 million or more annually on recruiting. Boise State's recruiting budget for all men's athletic programs in 2007 was $228,000, only fourth of the nine WAC teams, while Idaho, the last place team in the conference for the year in football, had the highest at $352,000. In fact, thirty-five of the fifty-two non-BCS conference teams generated higher recruiting expenses than BSU in the same year.

Considering the gross revenues from ticket sales for elite programs, $1 million allocated for recruiting expenses is small relative to their total budgets. Ohio State had an expense and debt service for football in 2006 of $33 million, but generated $61 million from ticket sales for a tidy profit of $28 million. 2006 National Champion Florida, in the same year, had an even better operating profit of more than $32 million. Oklahoma established a total football budget of nearly $14 million and paid head coach Bob Stoops in excess of $3 million. Boise State, with only an average budget for the WAC (San Jose State had football expenses of $4.6 million in 2007), spent about $3.4 million for football in 2006.

Winning and tradition are not the only attraction for starry-eyed eighteen-year-old prospects. The lavish facilities at major and even some mid-major programs are a draw in and of themselves. The University of Oregon, with whom Boise State commenced a home and home series beginning in 2008 and owners of one of the most modern all-around athletic facilities in the Pac-10, opened its $10 million Athletic Medicine Center in the fall of '07. The 15,000-square-foot complex with oak floors and smoked glass walls is a technological marvel. There are twenty-five massage tables, multiple therapeutic pools with underwater treadmills, state-of-the-art digital x-ray technology, hot-plunge cold-plunge pools, a pharmacy, and most important of all, a seemingly endless number of plasma TVs throughout the building.

Boise State's fellow WAC members Nevada and Fresno State don't take a back seat to anyone when it comes to strength, conditioning and physical therapy facilities. The Wolf Pack boasts of owning the best training facilities in the conference and one of the best in the West. The Bob & Nancy Cashell Football Center and the Primm Medicine and Strength facilities are superior to those at Boise State and compare favorably to the best in the Pac-10 and the MWC. Fresno State possesses the best campus stadium complex, and the strength and conditioning center is the newest and largest in the WAC.

Former Bronco defensive tackle Tony Altieri remembers that he made it a point to arrive at the training room for taping at least an hour earlier than other players before games, or risk not finding a place to sit because of limited room. Space was so scarce there were not enough meeting rooms when the positions split up to meet with their coaches. During most of the years Altieri played, the defensive linemen met in the band storage room.

The press box facilities above the west stands of Bronco Stadium were housed in essentially the same structure that was originally built in 1970 until the fall of 2008. Shortly after the Broncos joined the WAC an assistant coach from a conference member in the Southwest was said to have described the press box as the most austere he'd ever seen for a D-I program. As coach Chris Petersen toured the newly completed state-of-the-art press and premium seating Stueckle Sky Center, finished just in time for the 2008 opening game, he jokingly offered that it replaced the worst press box in America.

Until the football season of 2006, and completion of the first field house, the only full-sized practice field on the Boise State campus was the blue AstroPlay surface of Bronco Stadium. With no permanent non-synthetic practice field on campus, the team still uses off-campus former junior high facilities for expanded space and natural grass. BSU's football operations and training facility were state of the art for a Division IAA program a quarter century ago. By D-I standards today, they are only average, still tucked between the seats in the south end zone of Bronco Stadium.

Gladiator

[1]According to *Rivals.com*, Boise State's best recruiting year prior to 2009, in terms of blue chip prospects, was 2007, when seven three-star players signed letters of intent. Washington State University, dead last in the Pac-10 for recruit ratings in the same year, signed

---

1 Rivals.com uses a point system for ranking recruit classes for all FBS teams. Values are assigned to each recruit from the player's rating number, position rank and star ranking. Points are awarded to teams through a formula that rewards them for both the quantity of recruit commitments and the quality of those players.

twice as many three-star prospects at fourteen and added a four-star. The University of Oregon was rated the eleventh best recruiting class of all FBS teams in '07 (second only to USC in the Pac-10), signing twelve three-star and twelve four-star players.

[2]With cumulative annual recruit rating points below only those of USC and Cal of the Pac-10 since 2004 and through 2008, under *Rivals'* rating system, Oregon didn't surprise many when they beat WSU by forty-nine points in their 2008 matchup. What was a big surprise to most is that a top-twenty nationally ranked Oregon (No. 12 by USA Today), with a cumulative total of 91 blue chip players (including two five-stars and thirty four-stars) since the recruiting seasons of 2004 and ending in 2008, was defeated at home by unranked (before the game) Boise State, with a cumulative total of 23 blue chip players (one four-star and the rest three-stars) over the same recruiting period.

Boise State opened the 2009 season against number sixteen Oregon with its highest *Associated Press* pre-season ranking in history at number fourteen. The Ducks were still licking their wounds from the '08 loss to the Broncos and entered the contest promising to exact revenge with the consensus best quarterback in the Pac-10 Jeremiah Masoli, and elite running back LeGarrette Blount.

---

2 Adding up the *Rivals.com* annual points for a team over a specified period generates a cumulative ranking. This is not an official ranking given out by *Rivals*, but it is my way of determining the rankings for teams over a period of two or more recruiting seasons. This would seem the most logical manner in which to rank the prospect values of teams over a specified number of years.

In a game billed as the biggest regular season home game in school history, Boise State left no doubt in anyone's mind as to which was the better team. The final score was 19–8, but the relatively narrow point spread didn't reflect the Broncos' dominance. With a young starting defense that included only two *Rivals.com* blue chip (both three-stars) recruits from high school and four sophomore replacements for five of the departed seniors from 2008, BSU held Masoli and Blount to a combined net 9 yards rushing and completely overwhelmed the Ducks. Oregon was without a first down until the third quarter, ended the game with only six to BSU's twenty-two first downs, and could muster only 152 yards of total offense against the Broncos' balanced 361.

The story of quarterback Kellen Moore, a member of the Boise State 2007 incoming freshman class, seems only to confirm Bronco head coach Chris Petersen's belief that what he describes as blue collar recruits can compete with teams stocked with higher rated players. After only four games and four wins in 2008, Moore, just a redshirt freshman, collected the sixth best rating of all FBS quarterbacks, a national player of the week award after the Oregon game, and two WAC offensive player of the week awards.

Moore, however, was only the fourth ranked quarterback in his home state of Washington by *Rivals* at the end of his senior year in 2006, and just the tenth-rated player overall.

So what did all those prospects ranked ahead of Moore do after they left high school? Eight players were offered scholarships and signed with Pac-

10 teams, while a ninth received a scholarship and signed with perennial mid-major power BYU. Moore received only two FBS scholarship offers, one from Boise State and one from Idaho.

Of the three prototype size/arm quarterbacks (all between 6 foot 3, 209 pounds and 6 foot 5, 230 pounds) rated ahead of Moore (6 foot, 186 pounds), one could not qualify academically, one was converted to linebacker and then to tight end, and one decided to go on a Mormon mission after his redshirt season. While Moore, in only his third game as a starter, was decimating what many analysts called one of the best defensive secondaries in college football for 386 yards and three touchdown passes at sold out Autzen Stadium in Oregon, less than a handful of players ranked ahead of him out of high school from his home state had even made his team's two-deep roster and played in a college game.

NUMBER ONE

My uncle Bill often uncorked some notoriously great expressions. For example, when referring to a highly unusual occurrence, he would say, "Even a monkey falls out of a tree once in a while." I'll never forget the couple of years the great Hall of Famer Willie McCovey played for the San Diego Padres late in the twilight of his career. My uncle and I were season ticket holders, so we went to many games during the seventies.

For those who are not familiar, when Willie came to bat, the infielders and outfielders would perform the "McCovey shift" to anticipate the fact that the left handed batter almost always pulled the ball to the right side. The first baseman would play the right field line, the second baseman moved to short right field, the third baseman backed into short left field, and the outfield shifted so that the left fielder ended up in left center.

We were at San Diego Stadium on a pleasant summer evening watching the Padres when Willie came to bat. After the defense performed "The Shift," McCovey promptly fouled two pitches down the first baseline as if on cue. With two strikes, he was now attempting to protect the plate when the opposing pitcher threw a slider that had Willie completely fooled. As the ball was breaking off the outside corner of the plate, he tried to stop a reflex swing, but the ball shot off the end of his bat like a bullet just inside the left field foul line, devoid of any defensive players. The ball rolled all the way to the left field corner where, unbelievably, the third baseman and the left fielder converged at roughly the same time. McCovey was never known for his running speed even in his early years, so what would have surely been an inside the park homerun for almost any other player, became his only triple that year. For the first time I heard my uncle observe, "Well, even a monkey falls out of a tree once in awhile."

SEC vs. the World

A monkey fell out of a tree, so to speak, a few times during the 2007 college football season, i.e. Appalachian State shocked Michigan, and the University of Louisiana Monroe mugged Alabama, to name a couple. During the 2008 regular season, several mid-majors flexed their muscles and knocked off BCS teams; BYU and Utah from the Mountain West Conference, Boise State, and Fresno State from the WAC, and East Carolina from Conference USA all beat BCS Conference teams and jumped into or up the national rankings.

2009 produced more history-making mid-major upsets, beginning with Utah's domination of Alabama in the January 2 Sugar Bowl game. Opening week of the '09 regular season was no less spectacular for an underdog non-BCS team, when BYU rocked number three ranked Oklahoma 15–14. BYU's fellow Mountain West Conference member Colorado State rounded out the weekend with a victory over what was supposed to be a rebuilt Big-12 Colorado team.

Upsets by mid-majors over BCS conference teams may garner headlines, but they are a rare occurrence in college football, and for obvious reasons. Most BCS teams clearly possess rosters full of better quality players. For example, from 2002 through 2008, *Rivals.com* gave only three current non-BCS teams a recruit class ranking in the top fifty; BYU ranked thirty-sixth in '02, San Diego State had classes ranked forty-eighth and forty-sixth in '03 and '04, respectively, while Southern Mississippi had classes ranking forty-sixth in '02 and thirty-seventh in '08.

In mid-January 2007, and following the major bowl games, the president of the University of Georgia, Michael Adams, decided to present his case for an eight team playoff to the NCAA. If that wasn't enough for Bulldog fans, the Georgia state legislature introduced a resolution backing Adams. At the same time, USC backers and the Southern California media were also clamoring for a playoff.

The earnest statements from Georgia and USC resulted from each party's frustration with a BCS system that effectively eliminated them from an opportunity to play for the national championship when both teams lost two games during the regular season. The ire of both sides toward the BCS system was exacerbated by the fact that LSU, the eventual national champion, also had two losses. Both camps seemed confident that with dominating wins over opponents in BCS Bowl games, (Georgia a 41–10 win over Hawaii and USC a 49–17 win over Illinois), they were at least on the same level as LSU.

Fans, media, and alumni had their stake in a playoff, but the head coaches for USC and Georgia voiced pangs of regret for not qualifying for the championship game because they had both spent a great deal of time, effort, and money to secure the very best football players in America.

According to *Rivals.com*, from 2002 through 2007, USC was head and shoulders above the rest of the FBS field in the competition to recruit the best players. Georgia was no slouch ringing in with the sixth best cumulative class ratings over the same period. USC maintained a significant lead over everyone in terms of high ranking classes with three number one's, a number two and a number three, while every Georgia recruit class ranked in the top ten.

When Southeastern Conference coaches gather for the annual media days event, they invariably proclaim their own as the preeminent conference for football in the country. After closer scrutiny of the player values for a majority of the teams in the SEC, it appears their claim might be a valid one.

Using *Rivals.com*'s annual point system for ranking recruiting classes and then gathering the cumulative totals for every FBS team from the '02 season through '07, the SEC boasts seven teams in the top-fifteen; Florida, LSU, Georgia, Tennessee, Auburn, South Carolina and Alabama. USC was the lone Pac-10 team in the top fifteen, while the ACC (Florida State and Miami), Big-12 (Oklahoma and Texas), and the Big-10 (Michigan and Ohio State) delivered two members each.

A reasonable thesis as to why the SEC separates itself from the other conferences in the power ratings is the fact it recruited 30 percent of all five-star players available since 2002 and through 2007. Unlike the other BCS conferences, where as few as one or two teams in the conference recruited most, if not all, of the elite players, the distribution among SEC conference members was much more balanced. For example, Florida and Tennessee tied for the largest percentage of five-star players at 25 percent of the total each, with LSU at 16 percent and Georgia at 10 percent. All of the other SEC teams except Vanderbilt and Kentucky reflected a distribution of from 8 percent to 2 percent of the total.

Compare the distribution of elite players in the SEC to that of the Pac-10 and you find a much different outcome. USC recruited 10 percent (twenty-five) of all elite players and significantly more than second place Florida and Tennessee (6 percent and fifteen players each). Compared to the rest of the Pac-10 teams, however, USC signed a lopsided 57 percent of the five-stars who came to the conference. The drop-off to number two was drastic, with UCLA recruiting only five elite players, or 11 percent of the total for the Pac-10.

If Pac-10 fans and coaches feel compelled to enter the battle of words and proclaim their conference as the best for football in the nation, they may want to consider where their prospects rank compared to those of the SEC. Again, using *Rivals.com* to determine annual rankings, and then adding the point totals over the same six years, the University of California had the second ranked recruiting classes in the Pac-10, but would have only finished eighth (nineteenth of all FBS teams) and just ahead of Arkansas in the SEC. There is, of course, a price to be paid for such high ranking recruits: the SEC schools generated the highest expenses, at more the $13 million in '06-'07 for general athletic recruiting, outspending the Pac-10 by $5.2 million.

With seven of the twelve SEC members finishing in the top fifteen of all teams in cumulative annual recruit ratings from '02 through '07 (no other conference had more than two teams finish in the top fifteen), the SEC can point to the balance of talent in the conference as evidence that they are certainly number one in that category. Furthermore, LSU, Georgia, and Auburn finished in the top seven in winning percentage from years '03 through '07, Tennessee and Florida finished in the top twenty over the same period. Add to that the national championships won by LSU (two) and Florida (two) since 2000 and through 2008, there appear to be some very good arguments that the SEC holds the quality cards so far in the twenty-first century.

Commentators often remind us that parity exists in college football today, and it's true that there was a slight leveling of the playing field when the NCAA mandated a maximum of eighty-five scholarships (down from ninety-five) per Division-I team in 1992. However, the most talented players are still committing to an exclusive group of schools. As mentioned, 40 percent of the five-star recruits between '02 and '07 were from ten SEC teams and USC. Another 31 percent (seventy-two) of the elite recruits went to traditional powers Texas, Oklahoma, Ohio State, Michigan, Penn State, Florida State, Miami, and Notre Dame. That's 71 percent of the win/loss-influencing players concentrated primarily on 14 percent of all FBS teams.

In the BCS realm, the paradox of the argument "better players create better teams" may be Virginia Tech of the Atlantic Coast Conference. From 2002 through 2007, Florida State's classes ranked fourth overall and Miami's ninth, while both acquired four classes each rated in the top ten during the period. Virginia Tech's highest ranked class between the six years was fourteenth and the cumulative ranking of all classes was twenty-sixth.

The advantage Florida State and Miami enjoyed over Virginia Tech, with respect to the ratings of recruited players, can also be appreciated in the difference of highly rated prospects signed by the schools. FSU, with sixty-nine, and Miami at fifty-eight, both held considerably more high-star (four-star and five-star) blue chips compared to Virginia Tech's twenty-seven.

Virginia Tech joined the ACC in 2004, won the conference championship with the best record, and then played in the ACC championship game three times, with two wins, from '05 through '08. During the same span of five years the Hokies produced a winning percentage of .77612 (eleventh among all FBS schools), while Miami and FSU were thirty-seventh (.59677) and thirtieth (.62500) respectively. Virginia Tech's success seems to suggest that player development and coaching can occasionally make up for recruits of apparent lower quality.

Superman

By the time he was a senior at Mission Viejo High School in Southern California, Marty Tadman had become one of the best combination wide receiver/defensive backs in Orange County. Not blessed with great size or even breakaway speed, Tadman was, nonetheless, an extraordinary athlete.

He possessed a self-confidence that bordered on arrogance, modeling almost perfectly the stereotypical prep super jock. More destructive than this relatively benign personality flaw was his substance abuse. By age fifteen, he was a heavy drinker, smoker, and cocaine user, and at sixteen, a marijuana dealer.

Considering his assortment of addictions, it's a wonder Tadman was able to perform so well on the football field. Somehow he concealed the off-field behavior, and during his senior year of 2003 received several college scholarship offers.

He visited the campuses of two Pac-10 programs, but dismissed the locations as not to his liking. Surprising many, he took an official recruiting trip to Boise, fell in love with the city and accepted the Broncos' scholarship offer. When the coaching staff got wind of a partying episode during his trip, it did not sit well with them, and he was forced to explain himself to head coach Dan Hawkins or risk losing his free ride offer.

But for a spiritual encounter on a Southern California beach in April of 2004, Tadman may have languished in his drug dependence. After arguing with some friends at a Saturday night party, he drove to the beach by himself. As he strode along the water's edge in near total darkness, he had the impression that God was telling him to stop his drug abuse and seek him.

Within a few days of his divine encounter, Marty began reading the Bible in earnest, surrendered his life to Jesus Christ, and gave up his array of intoxicants cold turkey.

Tadman was one of a small group of recruits in the 2004 class to have received a scholarship offer from another FBS school other than Boise State, and the only one considered to be of blue chip quality. With unusual natural instincts and an uncanny ability to read offenses, he made an immediate impression on the coaches in the fall camp of his true freshman season.

Marty expected to spend his freshman year on the scout team as a redshirt, but injuries at the defensive back position forced Hawkins to play him in the fifth game of the season, against Hawaii. He rewarded his coach with an interception in that game, and though he played sparingly over the balance of the season, he established a foundation that would allow him to be a starting safety for the next three years.

Tadman garnered All-WAC honors three years in a row and became the national leader in career interceptions for current players. In the 2007 Fiesta Bowl, he was nearly flawless in his play and made two key interceptions: one saving a touchdown, and another allowing him to score a touchdown. For his superior play, he was named Fiesta Bowl defensive player of the-game.

WHO ARE THESE GUYS?

I live with my family in the Southwestern Riverside County bedroom community of Murrieta, California. Our little corner of the world is situated in the rolling hills, wine country of the Temecula Valley, about sixty miles north and inland from San Diego. The summers are warmer and much less overcast than the coastal communities, but easily ten to fifteen degrees cooler on average than the low desert temperatures. A natural on-shore air flow from the Pacific Ocean, about thirty miles to the west, passes over several hundred square miles of sparsely populated terrain, keeping our valley pristine and mostly smog-free year round.

In mid-November 1997, the first round of the Southern Section, California Interscholastic Federation (SS, CIF) football playoffs were beginning. Our Murrieta Valley High School Nighthawks, where my daughter was a cheerleader, were playing Claremont High School, from the eastern edge of Los Angeles County. We had an excellent team that year and, based on a high seeding, expected to win our first playoff game rather easily.

Claremont won the pregame coin toss and elected to receive the opening kickoff. Our excellent kicker booted the ball to about the five yard line, where the single kick return specialist stood for Claremont. The return man caught the ball on the fly and with a series of jukes and a burst of speed sprinted ninety-five yards for a touchdown.

Our comfort level returned to normal when, after a quick two-minute drive, the Nighthawks marched into the end zone and tied the game. Our coach wasn't born yesterday, so on the next kick-off, he directed the kicker to aim the ball away from the deep return man. The ball bounced to the thirty yard line and was picked up by a slow player who was almost immediately tackled.

The first play from scrimmage for Claremont was a post pattern pass to the only player to line up as a wide receiver. The young man simply ran past and beyond every defensive player, caught the ball in stride, and raced seventy yards for the touchdown.

We took a closer look at the number on his jersey and realized that it was the same player who had run the kickoff all the way for a touchdown. All of us reached for our programs to identify the young man, and from that moment to the end of the game, we remembered his name and number. Fortunately, he was the most talented player on an average team, and, for the most part, the defense was able to keep him under wraps for the balance of the game.

Two years later, I watched Boise State play in its first Humanitarian Bowl and initial postseason game as a Division I member. From the comfort of my home—the announcers said the temperature at kickoff was twenty-two degrees in Boise—I was entertained by what would be ESPN's most watched bowl game of the season. With ten lead changes, the Broncos out dueled Louisville to win 34–31.

A few plays into the game, BSU quarterback Bart Hendricks threw a long pass to wide receiver Lou Fanucchi. I remembered the name from somewhere, so after the game, I checked out the player roster on the BSU Web site. Sure enough, it was Lou Fanucchi from Claremont High School, the same player I had watched two years earlier in a high school game sprint to long touchdowns the first two times he touched the football.

The following year, I would have the opportunity to watch Fanucchi in the H-Bowl in person. He became Boise State's big play and leading receiver in 2000, averaging just slightly less than twenty yards per catch. Like almost every player on the BSU roster, he was lightly recruited out of high school.

Blue Chip vs. Blue Collar

From the time Rufus and Gerald Alexander began their careers in 2002 and finished in 2006, according to *Rivals.com*, Oklahoma recruited nine five-star prospects to Boise State's none, sixty-three four-stars to BSU's one, and forty-three three-stars to BSU's twelve. The recruiting service listed 121 scholarship recruits for Oklahoma during the period, of which four were two-star rated (3 percent of total recruits), while BSU listed 102 scholarship players, of which eighty-nine were two-star rated (87 percent of total recruits). Using *Rivals'* point system as the measurement for determining rankings of annual recruit classes, during the same five recruiting seasons, Oklahoma's point accumulation generated the third best overall ranking of all FBS schools, whereas Boise State placed seventy-ninth.

Another picture of the dramatic difference between the levels of talent attracted to the two programs appears in a comparison of NFL draftees (not including free agents). Between April draft years of 2003 and 2007, Oklahoma produced twenty-six NFL drafted players, including six in the first round and five in the second round, while Boise State had a total of six draftees, with two of those in the second round.

In 2002, when Rufus and Gerald signed letters of intent, according to *Rivals.com*, Oklahoma generated the seventh-rated recruiting class in college football and was one of only two D-I schools to sign exclusively blue chip players. The breakdown included the following: three five-star players, thirteen four-stars (the most of any school in '02) and eight three-stars. Every player who signed a letter of intent to Oklahoma that year received additional scholarship offers from other BCS universities. In addition to Rufus Alexander, nine Sooner Fiesta Bowl seniors, including quarterback Paul Thompson (four-star) and inside linebacker Zach Latimer (five-star), were part of the '02 recruiting class.

BSU, which owned the seventy-fourth rated class in '02 with no blue chip prospects, recruited the nucleus of its future Fiesta Bowl seniors including Gerald Alexander, linebackers Korey Hall and Colt Brooks, wide receivers Drisan James and Legedu Naanee, defensive back Quinton Jones, fullback Brad Lau, defensive tackle Andrew Browning, defensive end Mike G. Williams, and quarterback Jared Zabransky. Of these ten key players (nine starters, Jones was a kick and punt return specialist and backup cornerback), only Alexander, Naanee and Zabransky received scholarship offers from another FBS school, while Brooks and Browning were walk-ons, so neither of their names appeared in any of the recruiting services' databases.

Previous major bowl games have produced their share of "on-paper" mismatches, but nothing akin to the disparity between the '07 Fiesta Bowl participants. Oklahoma has the most national championships and wins of any football program in America since WWII (three national championships while the future Boise State University was still a junior college during the fifties), a home stadium capacity of 84,000 that dwarfs

BSU's 33,000, and a 2006 football budget of $14 million to BSU's $3.4 million; Bob Stoops' salary alone would have required most of Boise State's entire football budget in 2006.

When Fiesta Bowl Fox TV commentator Thom Brennaman used the David and Goliath analogy to describe the tradition, talent, and program resources gap between Boise State and Oklahoma, even that characterization may have understated the differences.

The Natural

If Bart Hendricks ignited the flames, Ryan Dinwiddie threw gasoline on the Boise State inferno. Dinwiddie was a slender, slightly over 6 foot, and maybe 175 pound classic drop-back passer from Elk Grove, a suburb of Sacramento, California. In his career as starting quarterback, he was successful in leading Elk Grove High School to a 27–1 record.

However, he didn't have success convincing a major university to overlook his relatively small stature and offer him a scholarship. Though Dinwiddie displayed great position presence and a strong, accurate arm in high school, he was well under the size minimum for major college programs. For strong-armed, relatively immobile pocket passers, coaches wanted quarterbacks like his contemporaries Phillip Rivers, Eli Manning, Ben Rothlisberger, and, from his own conference, David Carr, all ranging in size from 6 foot 3, 220 pounds to 6 foot 5, 240 pounds. Dinwiddie's scholarship option was Boise State.

Dinwiddie shouldered added burdens in 2001 as he took over the starting reins from Bart Hendricks. He was coming in at the same time Boise State was entering its first season in the upgraded Western Athletic Conference and with the most difficult schedule in the school's five year Division-I history. In addition, his drop-back style contrasted with Hendricks's improvisation and mobility.

Fortunately, head coach Dan Hawkins had just hired a bright young offensive coordinator and quarterbacks coach from the University of Oregon by the name of Chris Petersen. Petersen and Dinwiddie were able to start their BSU careers at the same time, and the results of mentor and student were nothing short of spectacular.

If 1999 through 2001 were the precursor to Boise State's meteoric rise to national prominence, the next two seasons under the quarterback leadership of Ryan Dinwiddie brought the program to full bloom.

In 2002 and 2003, the Broncos would record twenty-five wins, including two bowl victories, and for the first time in their short history as a Division I participant be ranked twelfth and fifteenth, respectively, in national polls at the end of each season. During the two-year period, only a pair of losses blemished a perfect record, and both of those were travel games against BCS and bowl-qualifying teams, Arkansas (2002) and Oregon State (2003). The Oregon State game was a 24–26 loss at Corvallis, where after a crucial play at the end of the contest, placement of the ball by Pac-10 officials may have cost Boise State the win.

The bowl wins in both years gave indication of just how far the Broncos had progressed with a 33–16 victory over BCS team Iowa State and its future NFL quarterback Seneca Wallace in the Humanitarian Bowl, and a hard-fought win against nationally ranked, eleven-game-winning TCU in the Fort Worth Bowl.

Ryan Dinwiddie may have been small in stature compared to his larger quarterback contemporaries, but on the football field he was more than a match for every one of them. When the game clock stopped at the end of the Fort Worth Bowl, Dinwiddie owned the Division I all-time career passing efficiency record of 168.19. He re-wrote nearly all the passing records at Boise State as a three-year starter, and his 9,819 career passing yards might be even more remarkable when one considers that he missed four games with a broken leg in '02 and BSU featured a balanced run/pass offense with the leading rusher in the conference, tailback Brock Forsey, in '01 and '02. During his senior year, he passed for 4,356 yards, not to blue chip, future NFL wide receivers, but mostly to a pair of diminutive 5 foot 9, former walk-ons, Tim Gilligan and T.J. Acree.

IN THE BEGINNING

In 1998, after a third consecutive lopsided win by the University of Nevada Reno over the Broncos, it was reported that the Wolf Pack coaching staff boasted that if Boise State didn't improve the quality of its players, they saw no reason to continue the rivalry. With a six-game winning streak, it appeared as if Nevada might be on the verge of duplicating domination over the Broncos that had already been achieved by the University of Idaho starting a decade and a half earlier.

Whether or not the succession of head coaches has instilled a unique motivation in the players towards it, the "rivalry" has been dominated by Boise State since 1999. Like all of the other teams in the old Big West Conference and the new Western Athletic Conference, Nevada has borne the brunt of the improved "quality" of BSU players. Between the seasons of 1999 and 2008, Boise State and Nevada played nine times, the Broncos winning all nine and most by lop-sided scores.

Where do they Rank?

With Boise State's rapid ascension to the top ranks of Division I mid-major football, one might assume that the Broncos' brain trust of coaches far outpaced the other conference members when it came to luring top-rated talent. What other explanation could there be for a win-loss record of 108–20 since 1999 (the best in the FBS through 2008), the highest points per game average since 1999 for all FBS members (40.5 through the '08 regular season), fifty consecutive regular season home wins (best in the FBS since '99), 70–5 conference record since '99 (best in the FBS since '99), five season ending top-twenty-five national rankings since 2002 and through 2008 (the most of any non-BCS teams over the same period), ten or more wins in eight seasons since 1999 and through 2008 (tied for the most in FBS), eight conference titles along with two runners-up since '99, and nine bowl appearances since 1999 and through 2008?

Rating the talent levels of high school and junior college football players is far from an exact science.

No rating service can project how an individual FBS prospect will perform at the next level, but it is obvious after several years of data collection that there is a correlation between the value (ranking) of a team's recruiting classes (as judged by the rating services) and its winning percentage over a period of time.

Rivals.com began publishing the ratings of players and teams in the early 2000s, and in the opinion of this writer, they provide some of the most consistent data available. Since much in the determination of a prospect's value is subjective, there will always be variances in how a player is viewed by one group of observers versus how the same player is judged by another group.

It will undoubtedly be pointed out, by those who observe the recruiting process closely, that in a few cases, prospects listed by rating services as having signed or committed to a program never, in fact, enrolled in school. For example, in 2005 *Rivals* shows Boise State signing six three-star or better players, when in reality two of those players never enrolled. The total number of scholarship commitments that year, according to *Rivals*, was sixteen, so the percentage loss of two three-star players would have made a significant difference in BSU's ranking and overall relationship to other conference recruiting classes.

In order to maintain conformity, all of Boise State's classes as listed by *Rivals.com* have been recorded, making no provision for players who may never have enrolled for one reason or another. Since it is likely that this same scenario existed with respect to listings for other teams, it must be understood that the data may be incomplete.

Beginning in 2002 Boise State was only seventh of all WAC teams in its recruit class ranking. In 2003, *Rivals* ranked BSU 101st of 120 FBS schools, and with one exception, every team in the Western Athletic Conference generated higher rated recruit classes than Boise State. The Broncos were ranked fourth in the WAC in 2004 and eighty-fifth of all FBS programs.

Boise State finally caught up with the top WAC teams, and in the recruiting seasons of '05, '06 and '07 enjoyed better point totals, and a slight ranking edge over the next three closest conference members each year. In 2008 the Broncos could generate no better than a fifth place ranking behind Fresno State, Hawaii, Louisiana Tech and Nevada.

Since the 2002 season and through 2008, the six WAC teams who have played full schedules against each other and in order of conference-only winning percentages are Boise State (.9642), Hawaii (.7142), Fresno State (.6607), Nevada (.5714), Louisiana Tech (.4821) and San Jose State (.3929). Using *Rivals'* data over the same span of years, the top five teams are only slightly separated from each other in terms of their accumulated annual team recruit value point totals: Fresno State (2,505), Hawaii (2,255), Boise State (2,244), Nevada (2,066), San Jose State (1,898) and La. Tech (1,460).

Adding up the three-star or better players recruited to each program over the period reveals that Boise State ranks third: Fresno State 36, Hawaii 29, BSU 25, Louisiana Tech 20 and Nevada 13. In '05, '06 and '07 when Boise State won the conference battle for highest ranking recruit classes, the Broncos were first, second (to Fresno State) and third (Hawaii first, Fresno State second) respectively in average star rating.

In the Pac-10 (USC), Big-12 (Texas & Oklahoma) and Big-10 (Ohio State & Michigan), where only one or two teams hold very large winning percentage margins over the rest of the teams in their respective conferences since 2002, those top teams also have significantly higher recruit values than the rest of the conference members. For example, USC owns the best conference-only winning percentage (.8814) and highest cumulative team recruit value point totals (17,866) in the Pac-10 since 2002. Cal with the second best winning percentage (.6101) has a point total of 9,321, followed in third position by Oregon with (.5932) and total points of 8,902.

UCLA accumulated the second best point total over the period at 9,737 and the fifth best conference-only winning percentage of all Pac-10 teams at .5254—affected largely by the three-win six-loss '08 season, but also may be reflective of poor utilization of high quality players. Stanford, with 4,885 points and separated by 12,981 points from USC (USC's total points were nearly 3.7 times Stanford's), owned the second worst recruit ranking of all Pac-10 members, while also generating the ninth place winning percentage. San Jose State with the worst conference winning percentage of the six WAC teams since 2002, totaled 1,898 recruiting points to BSU's 2,244—a difference of 346 points (Boise State's total points were 1.2 times those of San Jose State).

If nothing else, the exercise demonstrates that 1) USC enjoys the same commanding lead in winning percentage over its conference mates that Boise State has over the other members of the WAC, and 2) the Trojans have acquired significantly better players than the rest of the conference to achieve their margin of winning percentage in the Pac-10 than has Boise State to reach its margin of winning percentage in the WAC.

Though the data is open to debate on several accounts, while Boise State was winning fifty-four of fifty-six conference games and six WAC championships (five consecutive) in seven seasons between '02 and '08, it seems reasonable to conclude that the Broncos had nothing close to a distinct advantage with respect to prospect rankings over other WAC members as judged by at least one of the major recruiting services.

This hypothesis is further bolstered by the fact that since the 2001 season when the Broncos joined the WAC, they have sent only one player over the average (twelve) for the entire conference to the NFL as draftees or free agents. Furthermore, after the undefeated regular seasons of 2004 and 2008, not a single Boise State player was drafted by an NFL team in the following year's draft.

Division I at Last

Beginning in Boise State's initial Division I season of 1996 and through 1998, the preponderance of core players was only D-IAA quality. The win/loss record of 12–22 for the first three years was mostly attributable to the lower talent level, but a contributing factor had to be coaching turnover, with three different head coaches for the period.

Under the circumstances, the progression of wins per year was commendable at exactly two from 1996 through 1998 until 1999, when Boise State won its first of two consecutive Big West Conference titles, with a spike to ten wins. Progress of the program might have been revealed even more dramatically in 2000 by two BSU losses and one win. The only losses in the season were road games to BCS conference teams Arkansas and Washington State, both by only seven points. The win in the Humanitarian Bowl over Western Athletic Conference co-champions UTEP was a warning shot over the bow of the conference that Boise State would be one of its new members the following year.

If BSU was at a distinct disadvantage in terms of player talent from its beginning as a D-I program in the Big West Conference, how could it compete with the more tradition laden universities from the Western Athletic Conference? Every school in the new WAC had many more years of experience as a four-year program, larger alumni base, and longer Division I participation.

The two flagship WAC programs in 2001 from the West, Hawaii and Fresno State, were steeped in tradition by comparison. Both became Division I members shortly after Boise State began playing four-year football. Just ten years earlier, in 1991, Hawaii won the

WAC championship, beating Illinois in the Holiday Bowl, while in the same year Fresno State defeated USC in the Freedom Bowl. Both teams came from cities considerably larger than isolated Boise and played in stadiums with much greater capacities.

In addition to Hawaii and Fresno State, the evolving new conference included Tulsa and the University of Texas El Paso along with former Southwest Conference members Southern Methodist and Rice. All of these schools enjoyed four-year football dating back to the 1910s, Division I affiliation from the 20s, 60s and 70s, and a string of household name NFL players. San Jose State spawned future NFL coaching greats Bill Walsh and Dick Vermeil and also produced a rich tradition of offensive football, ruling the Division I Pacific Coast Athletic Conference/Big West Conference from 1975 to 1992 with eight conference championships and the fourth best winning percentage among mid-majors over the period. Louisiana Tech, a D-IAA powerhouse for years, joined the ranks of D-I in 1989. Even former Big Sky and Big West conferences rival Nevada started playing four-year football thirty-one years before BSU and preceded the Broncos to Division I by four.

Some critics argue that the WAC was a weak conference when Boise State entered in 2001, but a closer examination of the members in the top half reveal some highly competitive teams. Fresno State, Louisiana Tech, Hawaii, and Rice had a combined win loss record of 35–15. Fresno State and Louisiana Tech both participated in bowl games and played very demanding schedules, including four BCS teams each. Fresno State beat three BCS teams to start the season, including eventual Big 12 Conference winner Colorado on the road, and was ranked as high as eighth in a national poll. Hawaii, at 9–3, dominated a previously unbeaten, 12–0, top-ten ranked Mountain West Conference champion BYU by a score of 72–45, and Rice had one of its best teams in twenty-five years with a record of 8–4; one of its losses was to BCS team Nebraska.

If losses can give perspective to a team's quality, Boise State's first two games of its 2001 inaugural WAC season are noteworthy. The opener was a cross country trip against Lou Holtz' South Carolina Gamecocks, who would eventually compile a 9–3 record, beat Ohio State in a bowl game, and end the season ranked thirteenth in the AP poll. If that wasn't difficult enough, Washington State would make its first visit to Bronco Stadium for the next game. The Cougars, and possibly their most successful quarterback ever, Jason Gesser, ended the season ranked tenth with a 10–2 record (one of the losses to number two Oregon) and a win over Purdue in the Sun Bowl.

Consider several obstacles that Boise State would be required to overcome on the way to an 8–4, 2001 first WAC season.

- The breaking in of a new head coach.
- Loss of two-time conference MVP quarterback Bart Hendricks to graduation, replaced by an untested player.

- Traveled cross-country twice, across the Pacific Ocean once, and to California to play the best four teams in the conference.
- Defeated number eight-ranked and previously unbeaten Fresno State on the road against quarterback David Carr, the number one player taken in the NFL draft from that year.
- Beat Hawaii on the road against prolific passer Timmy Chang and wide receiver Ashley Lelie, Hawaii's all-time leading pass receiver in yards and touchdown receptions, and the nineteenth player taken in the draft the following year.

Few would have ventured to project in the preseason of 2001 that Boise State would, in its first year of play, boost the overall stature of the Western Athletic Conference by its mere presence. BSU was the conference co-runner-up at 6–2, and with eight total wins would be bowl-qualified by today's standards. Unfortunately for the Broncos, there were not as many bowl games available for WAC teams in 2001 as there are today. Louisiana Tech was the conference champion with an automatic invitation to the Humanitarian Bowl, while Fresno State with eleven wins and a guaranteed first round draft pick quarterback, was far more attractive to the Silicon Valley bowl committee than BSU.

If the best teams in the conference were going to beat Boise State, they needed to do it during the Broncos' theoretical developmental years. Unfortunately for the rest of the WAC, those years never existed, and only twice from 2002 through 2008 seasons did Boise State lose conference games. Both losses were road games against very good teams; Fresno State enjoyed eight first team All-WAC selections to Boise State's three in 2005 and twelve members of Hawaii's BCS Sugar Bowl team collected all-conference honors, compared to the Broncos' five in 2007.

Cool Hand Luke

Jim McMillan was raised in rural Canyon County about thirty-five miles west of Boise, and started his high school football career at the same time Boise State began to play four year football, in 1968. Like many Treasure Valley athletes of the time, without exposure and notoriety, his high school quarterbacking skills were not so pronounced that major college programs were willing to offer a scholarship.

BSU head coach Tony Knap, with an offense that emphasized passing, saw enough height at nearly, 6 foot 1, arm strength, throwing accuracy, and leadership qualities to consider McMillan a prime college quarterback prospect at any level. After McMillan's high school senior year of 1970, Knap offered him a scholarship to the fledgling four-year program and began the process of teaching his innovative offense.

McMillan was not the overnight success that many may have envisioned. Ron Autele, an athletic quarterback who could run, had a strong arm, and moved well in the pocket, was a year ahead of McMillan. Autele was the heir apparent to BSU's first great quarterback, Eric Guthrie, who had graduated in the spring of 1972. After showing signs of brilliance the previous season, Autele was hurt much of his junior year, allowing McMillan an opportunity to display his skills.

Autele and McMillan were very much opposites in demeanor and quarterbacking style. McMillan was the classic drop back passer whereas Autele was an athletic, dual-threat who often took much greater risk. With the injury to Autele, sophomore McMillan struggled to bring the offense into his fold. Beginning the 1973 season Autele, the senior, was officially the starting quarterback, but McMillan was finally ready to take charge. With his leadership skills and a genuine feel for Knap's offense, McMillan led Boise State to the top of Division II football.

During the ten-win '73 season, his top receiver, former Borah High School of Boise standout senior Don Hutt, who still holds the BSU career receptions record at 189, became an *Associated Press* First Team All-American, while McMillan was named the All Big Sky First Team Quarterback. In 1974 the McMillan-led Broncos won another conference championship and a second consecutive convincing win over the University of Idaho. He was voted the top Division II quarterback in the nation and a First Team AP All-American.

Jim McMillan set the standard for Boise State quarterbacks, and though his career passing statistics seem modest compared to more recent Bronco signal callers, he still ranks fifth for career passing yardage (through the '08 season) and second for touchdown passes in a season at thirty-three. He is third on the list for games with 300 or more passing yards in a career at seven and the only Boise State quarterback to throw for six touchdowns in one game.

MAGIC OF THE BLUE

I was called to a hastily arranged year-end meeting on December 30, 1998, at the Los Angeles high-rise headquarters of the regional brokerage firm where I worked. I enjoyed the good fortune of being able to work from my home office about one hundred miles removed from the smog and congestion of LA. When I arrived at the meeting a little tardy, not having planned for holiday traffic, I found the other senior officers huddled around the wide-screen TV in the CEO's office, watching a football game. It was not the first time, nor would it be the last that I would hear similar comments, when one of the observers pierced the air with, "Is that a freaking blue football field or am I seeing things?"

The Humanitarian Bowl, which had a mid-course sponsor change to MPC Computers Bowl, then a reversion back to the Humanitarian Bowl, was first played in 1997 and is currently billed as the longest running cold weather bowl game in America. The average high temperature for late December in Boise, Idaho, is thirty-five degrees and the low is twenty-two, so the "cold weather" moniker is well earned. It must have been late July when the H-Bowl committee gathered in an air conditioned office to determine a venue for showcasing Big West and, in the future, Western Athletic Conference football.

Surprisingly, the game has never been played in a full blizzard, but I did attend the 2000 edition where the temperature hovered close to freezing with intermittent snow. I'm a skier and had just visited the local ski area, Bogus Basin, so I was prepared, but the small contingent that followed the WAC co-champions, University of Texas El Paso, seemed as overwhelmed by the weather as their team was by BSU quarterback Bart Hendricks's outstanding MVP performance.

Maybe not a great number of bowl gazers across the country have whiled away hours watching the Humanitarian/MPC/ Humanitarian Bowl over the years, but they did get a glimpse of "The Blue." Even before the Fiesta Bowl media explosion, a mention of Boise State football would invariably elicit an, "Oh, that's where the blue field is."

The Man behind "The Blue"

In 1982, Gene Bleymaier, native Boisean and former UCLA star tight end from the early seventies, became Boise State's Athletic Director. The blue version of the field replaced the standard green AstroTurf in the summer of 1986, and it was Bleymaier who conceived the idea and carried through with the change. Almost everyone, including fans, administration, media, coaches, and even the manufacturer of AstroTurf, tried to talk him out of the color scheme, but Bleymaier stuck to his guns. In July of 1986, as he stood in the stands by himself, watching the first swaths of turf being laid, Bleymaier was slightly uneasy, especially since the manufacturer could not guarantee that the shade of blue would match the samples he ordered.

On September 13, 1986, the first game was played on "The Blue," when Boise State crushed Humbolt State 74–0. Many opponents, media, and fans have ridiculed the color, and a few years later, University of Idaho head football coach John L. Smith would call it "a desecration of the game." *Sports Illustrated* did a short story on the field after the first game and dubbed it the Smurf Turf. In a more recent local poll, the formerly fickle public gave an 80 percent approval to the blue color. The newest generation of synthetic turf, AstroPlay, installed in 2002, wore out more quickly than expected and was replaced in the summer of 2008 by a new manufacturer, FieldTurf.

Whatever one's personal bias toward the field color, it represents marketing genius, adding to the folklore that has become Bronco football. "The Blue" has also become a symbol of the blue-collar work ethic and an inducement for recruits to commit to the program. It is not at all unusual for a prospect to return home from an official recruiting visit to boast excitedly to his local media reporter that he walked on "The Blue" for the first time.

Gene Bleymaier's contribution to Boise State football goes well beyond his vision for a blue field; he might just be the most significant factor in the BSU equation of success. He pushed for entry into Division I when most Big Sky Conference teams were content with the status quo, conceived the plan for a local bowl game, rallied alumni and regional financial support and with limited resources and serious space constraints has overseen the building of the infrastructure that supports all facets of football operations.

Bleymaier is an energetic sort who, in his mid-fifties, still looks as if he could run a post pattern and leave tacklers in his wake. In the early nineties, he and then-university-president John Keiser cooked up the idea to elevate Boise State to Division I in football and join the open armed Big West Conference. Politics reared its ugly head, when a state board of education stacked with University of Idaho alums weren't about to let Boise State precede the flagship university for the state to D-I. The board axed the plan, and Keiser was summarily terminated for not fully disclosing information regarding actions he had taken in the process.

When the political climate changed by the mid-nineties, Bleymaier made his move and Boise State joined the University of Idaho in the Division I Big West Conference in 1996. After engineering the move to D-I and a short five-year stint with the Big West Conference, he smoothly transitioned the program to the WAC, ironically four years ahead of the University of Idaho's entry.

Boise State's six head coaches since 1993 and through 2009 give the appearance of excessive turnover. The reality is that only one of the coaches lost his job due to poor results. Pokey Allen took the Broncos to the 1994 D-IAA championship game in only his second year on the job, and was so popular that he might have coached until he retired, but he died unexpectedly of cancer. When Allen became ill in early 1996, Bleymaier appointed assistant coach Tom Mason as head coach for the inaugural season in the Big West Conference. Everyone hoped, though the prospects were slim, that Pokey would recover and eventually take back the reins of the head coaching position. After Allen's death in late December and a two win, ten loss season for Mason, Houston Nutt was hired to replace Mason. Nutt, who had been on a fast track to Arkansas, left for that vacant head coaching position at the end of 1997.

At year end 1997, Bleymaier had cause to be concerned; it was nearing the end of recruiting season, the program completed its first two years in Division I with a disappointing six wins, seventeen losses, and there was no head coach. If all of these challenges weren't enough to keep him awake at night, Bleymaier's assumption of the athletic director's duties coincided with the beginning of an embarrassing twelve-game losing streak against bitter upstate rival University of Idaho.

Fortunately, Bleymaier found an up and coming young offensive coordinator, Dirk Koetter, who came armed with a proven record of success at four major college programs and most recently the University of Oregon. For the third consecutive year and at the most critical juncture in school football history, fragile infancy in Division I, Boise State would start the season with a new head coach. If year-end 1997 supplied the darkest days for Bleymaier in his tenure as BSU's Athletic Director, the next decade would bring redemption for diligence and dedication.

1998 was the beginning of the renaissance for Boise State football. The Broncos enjoyed remarkable success in their beginning as a four-year program from the late sixties to the early eighties, but experienced a dark ages of sorts in the eighties and much of the nineties. The program generated its first Division I winning season in 1998 with a 6–5 record, losing a heartbreaker in overtime to Idaho. Since that year, however, the Broncos have dominated the series with a ten-game winning streak.

At the end of the 2002 regular season, with a first WAC championship followed by a bowl win against a BCS conference team, it was clear that Boise State had momentum. In 2003, Bleymaier and second-year head coach Dan Hawkins adopted the phrase "Brick by Brick—Building a Legacy" as their slogan for that year. By the end of the '03 season, with a school record-tying thirteen wins, a second WAC title, and a bowl victory over a ranked opponent, it was clear that there was not only a strong foundation, but a ton of bricks were stacked on Boise State's football program.

He would still be forced to replace his second coach to be enticed by a BCS program, but over the next five seasons the magic of Boise State was probably more than even the big dreamer, Gene Bleymaier, could have envisioned.

Major League

Whenever the subject of conversation between ex-high school jocks from Boise's Treasure Valley turns to the greatest athlete to originate from the state of Idaho, for those born before 1955 a pleasant interaction often becomes a debate that invariably narrows to two figures: Larry Jackson and Harmon Killebrew.

Killebrew probably has more national recognition since he became a Major League Baseball Hall of Famer and member of the exclusive "500" home run club. However, it would be wrong to discount Jackson. Playing in today's market at mid-career, with the numbers he produced in the fifties and sixties, Jackson would likely command a multi-year contract, paying $15 million annually.

Right-hander Jackson pitched for the St. Louis Cardinals, Chicago Cubs, and Philadelphia Phillies in a career that spanned fourteen years and produced a lifetime 194–183 win/loss record. His best year was 1964, when he was runner-up for the Cy Young award with a 24–11 record (most wins in the league) and a 3.14 earned run average.

Before Major League Baseball stardom, Jackson was an outstanding football player for Boise Junior College in 1949 and 1950. As a single wing tailback, equally adept at running as he was passing the ball, he led his teams to nineteen wins and only one loss during his junior college career.

At nearly 6 foot 2, 185 pounds, Jackson was almost always faster and usually bigger than most of the linebackers and defensive backs he played against. With excellent speed, a rocket throwing arm, and extraordinary athleticism, Jackson could take over football games all by himself.

After leaving Boise High School, where he was a basketball, baseball, and football star, he led the Broncos to their first postseason bowl game—the Potato Bowl in Taft, California, where they beat Taft Junior College 25–6. In 1950, the original Bronco Stadium was built and Jackson threw the first touchdown pass in the new stadium, to his brother Jerry in a game against Modesto Junior College.

At the end of the 1950 season, he and his undefeated team received a berth in the Junior Rose Bowl in Pasadena, California, where the Broncos lost their only game of the year to Long Beach City College in the national junior college championship game.

FOOTBALL IN THE GEM STATE

From 1968 through 1982, head coaches Tony Knap and Jim Criner combined for a stellar 130–40–1 record during the Broncos' first fifteen years as a four-year program. Even more surprising during that period was Boise State's domination of in-state rivals University of Idaho and Idaho State. Both of the other major universities had played four-year football since the turn of the twentieth century, and most observers expected BSU to absorb several years of drubbings by their upstate and cross-state foes before becoming competitive.

Instead, Boise State won its first three meetings with Idaho State and went on to a 13–2 record against the Bengals through the end of Criner's tenure. The Broncos didn't play Idaho until 1971, embarrassing a very good, Big Sky Conference champion, 8–3 Vandal squad 42–14 in the inaugural game. Boise State would lose the second game between the two by one point, then go on to win seven of the next nine (one tie), six with an average winning margin of twenty-seven points.

1982 was the beginning of the end of Boise State's dominance over the University of Idaho when Dennis Erickson, in his first year as head coach, brought the Vandals back from a previous year 3–8 record to beat the Broncos in a hard fought battle by seven points. Idaho turned the tables on Boise State from '82 through '98 with a 15–2 record and twelve consecutive wins. From 1983 through 1992, two BSU head coaches, Lyle Setencich and Skip Hall, produced a commendable record of 66–48, but never beat Idaho nor did they win a conference championship.

Borah High School

At the end of the 1961 football season, former University of Oklahoma assistant Dee Andros was named head coach at the University of Idaho in Moscow. Andros would only stay at Idaho for three years before he moved on to the head coaching position at Oregon State, but somehow in the seasons of '62 and '63, the crusty ex-Marine was able to convince the largest crop of the most talented high school football players in the southwestern part of the state, maybe ever, to play at the northern Idaho university.

Though the Vandals would only win eleven games in seasons '62 through '64, it is important to put the seemingly modest results into context. In the twenty-five seasons between 1938 and 1962, Idaho averaged slightly over two wins. In the four seasons prior to '63, Idaho won a total of six games and had an 0–13 record against Oregon, Oregon State, Washington, and Washington State. In all thirteen games the Pacific Coast Conference schools registered 464 points to Idaho's seventy-three.

Andros was able to mold a group of players, including six blue chip prospects from the Boise area, into a team that would win five games in 1963 against what are today known as Division I mid-major schools. In 1964, Idaho beat Washington State for only the fourth time in forty years and challenged Oregon and Oregon State with six-point and three-point losses, respectively. In 1965 a Vandal squad comprised exclusively of Andros recruits defeated a very good 7–3 WSU team and also lost three heartbreakers, one to Washington by 5 points, one to Oregon by 3 points and another to Oregon State by 2.

"The Great Pumpkin," Andros' affectionate moniker at Oregon State (due to his girth and penchant for wearing all-orange outfits), would use his recruiting acumen to pluck added gems for his new team in the fall of 1965. With help from former Boise High School football coach Ed Knecht, who was an assistant at OSU, Andros went back to the Boise area to recruit the three best players in the valley. Kent Scott from Boise High, Roger Cantlon from Caldwell High, and the blue chip plum, Steve Preece from Borah High School, would help make Andros a local Corvallis, Oregon, legend.

It would take thirty-three years before Oregon State finally exceeded the success of the 1967–68 seasons. OSU's 1964 team, coached by Tommy Prothro, had gone to the Rose Bowl, but it was the 1967 Beavers who went on to an unprecedented number seven Associated Press ranking and 7–2–1 record. OSU defeated the eventual national champions, number one USC and O.J. Simpson, number two Purdue on the road, Iowa, also on the road, and tied number two UCLA in Los Angeles, earning the title "Giant Killers." The 1968 team would go on to nearly the same success with a 7–3 record and a final number fifteen ranking.

The keys to Oregon State's success in '67 and '68 were the sprinter speed, intelligence, and strong arm of possibly the best of all the players ever recruited by Andros from the Treasure Valley. Steve Preece possessed all the skills needed to manage Andros' option offense, while he was complemented perfectly by former Treasure Valley high school rivals, offensive tackle Scott, and wide receiver Cantlon.

When Andros scored the recruiting jackpot the first time around for the University of Idaho, he went to the source of the best high school football teams in the state of Idaho, Borah High School in Boise. Future Vandal stars linebacker LaVerl Pratt (who played his freshman year at Boise Junior College), defensive back Jerry Ahlin, and linemen Ray Miller and Gary Grove all came from Borah, as did Boise State middle linebacker Steve Svitak, a former teammate of the four, who would become the first Boise State All-American in 1969.

Borah consistently produced some of the best high school football teams in the Pacific Northwest and proved it by regularly playing, and beating, the top teams from other border states in the sixties, seventies, and early eighties.

Head coach Ed Troxel, who started his duties at Borah when the school opened in 1958, enjoyed a nine-year record of 78–6–2 until he left to become an assistant coach at the University of Idaho in 1967. Troxel's successor, Dee Pankratz, continued to dominate Idaho and Northwest high school football for another fifteen years.

Troxel was one of the first high school coaches in the West to incorporate weight lifting into his football-training regimen. He also strongly recommended that all football players, unless supremely skilled in other spring sports, participate on the track team, for which he also served as head coach. Track and field participation not only kept football players on a fitness-training program in the off-season, but likely contributed to Borah's near domination of the state track meet every year during his tenure, a tradition that continued well beyond his departure.

Notre Dame head coach of the sixties and seventies, Ara Parseghian, and UCLA coach Tommy

Prothro regularly came to Borah to recruit. Before high school teams were ranked nationally, Parseghian reportedly told the local Boise media that Borah had teams as good as the best he had seen in the country. During the late sixties to the mid-seventies, the University of Idaho coaches were said to have visited the dorms and fraternity houses on occasion to recruit former Borah players as walk-ons when injuries piled up.

Idaho didn't introduce a state play-off system for high school football until 1979, but there was only one season in the seventies that Borah was not at or near the top of the polls. Borah won the inaugural play-off championship game in '79, played for but lost the championship game in '80, then dominated the '81 season with an undefeated championship team. In the same '81–'82 school year, the Borah boys won the state basketball tournament and the state track meet.

Borah provided a seemingly endless supply of disciplined and talented players to the Boise State roster from the late sixties through the early eighties, many of whom became stars, and even a few All-Americans. The 1971 team included four offensive linemen and one wide receiver who were all starters and former Borah players. Some of the standout players from that era included the previously mentioned Svitak, running backs Ken Johnson & Cedric Minter, offensive lineman Greg Phillips, and wide receivers Dennis Pooley, Mike Holton, and Don & Terry Hutt. Svitak ('69), Don Hutt ('73) and Terry Hutt ('77) were all *Associated Press* first team All-Americans and Minter was a third

('78) and second ('80) team All-American. Don Hutt, Holton and Minter were all three-time first team All-Big Sky picks.

One of the best Borah players during the seventies, future BSU athletic director Gene Bleymaier, accepted a scholarship to UCLA, where he became a star tight end.

INVINCIBLE

The young man injured his shoulder so severely that it appeared he might never play football again. In the mid-seventies, badly separated shoulders with torn ligaments were far more problematic than today's almost guaranteed relatively quick injury recoveries, with the benefits of advanced medicine. Even if surgery and/or rehabilitation was successful, it might be more than a year before the injury would sufficiently heal enough for him to play again.

Borah High School's Cedric Minter was being touted as the best high school football player in Idaho, playing for the strongest football program in the state on that Friday evening in early September, 1976. After star performances as a running back in his sophomore and junior years, this was to be the promising season that would lead to a scholarship from a major university.

Instead, after the first play in the initial game of his senior season, the 5 foot 10, 155 pound running back was being wheeled off the field on a gurney. Oklahoma, Oregon, and Kansas were all waiting with great anticipation to see how his senior season would progress but all immediately withdrew any hint of a scholarship offer. Cedric Minter was left to wonder if he would ever play football again.

Jim Criner was just beginning his new job as head coach at Boise State in the fall of 1976 after taking the reins from the highly popular and successful Tony Knap. When all the other college coaches dropped Cedric on the trash heap of forgotten prospects, Criner stood by his original commitment to offer Minter a scholarship.

Because Cedric didn't play the rest of the season, it seemed to many a high risk gamble to offer a scholarship to an undersized and physically damaged player who missed playing football his entire senior year. Minter, however, proved to be an incredibly fast healer, showing up at Boise State fall practice his freshman year of 1977, fit and ready to play.

Though Minter was on scholarship, he was not guaranteed special placement in the running back hierarchy, so he was obliged to start at the bottom of the order. However, by the time the season began, five running backs had been injured, leaving Fred Goode as the starter and Cedric as the back-up. Unbelievably, Goode was hurt in the second game of the season against Fresno State, thrusting Minter into the starting role.

Cedric Minter didn't just go on to play football at Boise State. He became one of the best running backs ever for the Broncos. He never played at more than 175 pounds, was a two-time All-American, and set every

Bronco rushing record, including 4,475 career rushing yards, a mark that still stands through the 2009 season. To top off his incredible career of personal accomplishments, he helped lead the 1980 team to the Division IAA national championship.

In the spring of 2009, Preston Minter, Cedric's son, and a local Boise Timberline High School standout utility player, accepted an invitation by Boise State head coach Chris Petersen to walk on.

A DYNASTY IN THE MAKING

Not many colleges that eventually attained Division I status are able to state that they began their football program as a junior college, moved to four-year grade as Division II, stepped up a level to Division IAA and finally jumped to Division I. Boise Junior College, founded in 1932, heralded a succession of winning seasons unmatched by any other junior college in the country from the end of World War II through 1967. Formerly an assistant coach, Lyle Smith became the head coach in 1947 and produced a twenty-year record (he did not coach in the '51 season due to military service) of 157–26–8 (.848), sixteen conference titles, five undefeated seasons, and a national junior college championship in 1958. Smith was a legend in his own time, albeit a regional one, who took mostly local high school players and molded them into disciplined teams.

Smith resigned at the end of the 1967 season to become athletic director and began the search for a new replacement. He promptly hired a former football teammate at the University of Idaho, highly regarded former Division I Utah State head coach Tony Knap, to lead the program into its new four-year status. Knap had been successful as both an assistant and head coach at Utah State and technically took a step down to coach Division II Boise State. Knap felt that the city of Boise and the college were not only well-placed to make a splash in Division II, but he had what seemed at the time the unfathomable vision of moving the program to Division I.

Former local Borah High School and Bronco running back from the early seventies, Ken Johnson, described Knap as an offensive genius. "We had a monstrous playbook with offensive schemes that none of us had ever seen or heard of before. He was able to figure out how to exploit weaknesses in every defense we came up against and sometimes would even invent new plays during the game, draw them up on the chalk board at halftime, and then run them in the second half." Johnson went on to say that when, for a few years, Knap couldn't find a quality tight end, he simply eliminated the position and added a running back.

Knap made it clear early at Boise State that he would emphasize the passing game, but not until his fourth season in 1971 were all of the player pieces in place so he could perform in dominating fashion. That year, in an era when only a few college teams passed more than ten or, at most, fifteen times per game, Bronco quarterback Eric Guthrie threw an average of twenty-eight times per game, totaled nineteen touchdown passes, and was only thirty-three short of 400 yards passing in one game. Johnson remembers Knap observing, "Why run the ball when you can pass it?"

Still the longest serving head coach for the program since 1968 at a relatively short eight years, Knap led the Broncos to a 71–19–1 record, three Big Sky Conference championships (Boise State was an independent for two of Knap's eight years as head coach), a new stadium, and a stadium expansion before leaving to take the head coaching position at University of Nevada Las Vegas.

Tough Act to Follow

As December, 2003, came to a close, the city of Boise was still basking in the afterglow of the most successful season in Boise State football history. With thirteen wins, a bowl victory at the home field of a nationally ranked team and a second consecutive year in the national rankings, no one wanted to look forward to a veteran-decimated team that was destined for a major rebuilding season in 2004.

Things degenerated in spring practice when the expected starting running back, senior Donny Heck, was declared academically ineligible. That left a little-used walk-on and a converted cornerback to duel for the starting position. At quarterback neither of the aspiring candidates was impressive or the clear winner in the final spring scrimmage duel to replace the prolific Ryan Dinwiddie.

If the stress of fielding what would be the second youngest football team in the FBS wasn't enough for coach Dan Hawkins to ponder in the off-season, the schedule for '04 listed consecutive early games against three very good teams: a veteran laden BCS Oregon State, a supremely talented University of Texas El Paso team under new coach Mike Price, and perennial Mountain West Conference power BYU.

The Broncos were coming off five seasons of unprecedented success. From the 1999 season through 2003, Boise State compiled the third best winning percentage in D-I with a record of 53–11, four conference titles and a runner-up, four bowl victories, and only one home loss. It was time for everyone to relax, allow the Broncos to take those anticipated knocks in '04, and rebuild for '05.

Magnum Force

Jared Zabransky was a rarity in today's one and occasionally two-sport focus athletes in high school. He favored basketball and baseball, but he also played football, if only for something to keep him occupied during the early fall months. Though he was an excellent athlete, with all-state awards in basketball and baseball, it didn't appear to recruiters that he possessed a particularly luminous talent to make him attractive enough for a college scholarship in any sport. He showed up at a Boise State football camp in the summer of 2001, prior to his senior year in high school, as an unknown quantity.

Almost immediately the Bronco coaching staff was so taken by Zabransky's speed and raw athletic ability that they offered him a walk-on opportunity. At the same time, the University of Idaho had been carefully eying him, got wind of his successful Boise State camp, and quickly offered a scholarship. With only a walk-on available at BSU, Zabransky made a verbal commitment to the Vandals. Head coach Dan Hawkins and his staff quickly re-evaluated their position and decided to make another effort to recruit Zabransky, only this time with a scholarship offer. He retracted his verbal commitment and signed a letter of intent to play at Boise State in February of 2002.

During the preseason fall camp of 2004, it was a forgone conclusion by local media and many fans that senior, three-year back-up Mike Sanford at 6 foot 4, 211 pounds and more prototypical size, would be the starting quarterback. Zabransky saw limited action as a redshirt freshman and completed a total of only eleven passes during the season. With young and, in several cases, unproven players at nearly every offensive position, it seemed logical that a veteran, fifth-year senior would be a good fit over the raw sophomore.

Zabransky was informed by coach Hawkins three days earlier, but not until he was the first quarterback under center on September 4, 2004, in the season opener against Idaho did the public realize he had been named the starter. The coach must have given a sigh of relief when his young quarterback rewarded him with eleven completions in sixteen passing attempts for 235 yards and three touchdown runs in a lopsided win over Idaho.

The next week Oregon State came to town, a team with the best receiver in the Pac-10, Mike Hass; 6 foot 6, 240 pound future NFL quarterback Derek Anderson; two all-conference cornerbacks; an all-conference offensive tackle; and Bill Swancutt, one of the best defensive end pass rushers in OSU history.

Make no mistake: Friday evening, September 10, 2004, was the biggest game in Boise State history. Admittedly, each of the four previous bowl victories was a monumental milestone along BSU's road to legitimacy as a Division I program, but the Broncos had never beaten a Pac-10 team in seven attempts, and Oregon State won the game in the previous year with the help of an official's mistake.

If Zabransky merely proved himself in his first starting role, with a national audience watching on ESPN, he and his Bronco mates were nothing short of spectacular against Oregon State. With sprinter speed, passing accuracy, and an ability to elude the rush, Zabransky showed a combination of skills never before displayed by a Bronco quarterback. He was 20–34 for 235 yards passing, three touchdown passes, seventy-three yards rushing, and one touchdown run. Boise State went on to skewer the Beavers 53–34.

Liberty is Her Name

The buzz started shortly after the 2004 regular season. The national media began to speculate about where the upstart, undefeated, and tenth ranked Boise State Broncos could find a prominent bowl game to showcase their number two nationally ranked scoring offense. The winner of the Mountain West Conference, Utah, was contracted to play the champion of Conference-USA, Louisville, in the Liberty Bowl. Seventh ranked Louisville had a powerhouse and its best team in history, though suffering a heartbreaking three-point loss to Miami during the regular season, or they would have been playing in a BCS bowl game and maybe even for the national championship. Utah, undefeated and by virtue of a higher computer-generated ranking than Louisville, was chosen as the first team from a non-BCS conference to play in a BCS bowl game.

Seizing the opportunity, the Liberty Bowl committee made an offer to Boise State in order to match the number one and number two scoring offenses in college football. BSU, however, as champion of the Western Athletic Conference, was by agreement obligated to play in the less-visible Humanitarian Bowl. A compromise was agreed upon with the H-Bowl committee, and conference runner-up Fresno State would play Atlantic Coast Conference representative, Virginia.

ESPN, having televised six Boise State games during the year, and *Sports Illustrated* featuring the Broncos in articles, including a two-page photograph of The Blue, offered complimentary exposure over the season that the program couldn't have imagined in its wildest dreams. The national media splash, along with the good fortune of having been selected to play in the more visible Liberty Bowl against a highly ranked opponent, could not have been scripted better for the Broncos.

Cinderella may not have married the prince, but the game lived up to its lofty billing by several sports writers and commentators as the best matchup of the bowl season. "It's a great way to end it," Louisville coach Bobby Petrino affirmed. "A national audience, two teams that were supposed to score eighty-four points. I think we hit it right on the top." With seven lead changes and the highest scoring Liberty Bowl in history, only a last second interception of a Jared Zabransky pass in the end-zone preserved a hard-fought 44–40 victory for the Cardinals.

Though it's doubtful that the Bronco coaches felt any consolation, this was a loss that ended in a marketing victory for Boise State. 2004 would end in an undefeated regular season and a bowl loss, but Boise State had garnered its third consecutive top-fifteen poll ranking, along with respect from the national coaching establishment, fans and college football media. It was time to look forward to the 2005 season opener with SEC power, Georgia.

BSU began the 2005 campaign with a pre-season national ranking for the first time in school history, and Zabransky was touted by *Sports Illustrated* as one of the fifteen "Gamebreakers" in college football. From the first play on offense at hot, humid Sanford

Stadium in Athens, Georgia, and 93,000 screaming Bulldog fans, Zabransky appeared overwhelmed. He would pitch four interceptions and lose two fumbles before he was mercifully pulled off the field for back-up Taylor Tharp in only the second quarter.

After the 48–13 pounding by Georgia, the Broncos would next lose a close three-point game when they allowed Oregon State a come-from-behind win in the last two minutes at Corvallis. Two more losses followed, to Fresno State and, finally, a furious comeback attempt against Boston College that fell just short with a last minute Zabransky interception in the MPC Computers Bowl.

Bronco faithful were somehow disappointed with a nine win, four loss season. Even though the team was plagued with several key injuries and the loss of starting defensive back Cam Hall for the first two games due to his suspension for an off-field incident, BSU fans placed most of the blame squarely on the shoulders of the quarterback. Many felt that the pressure to meet expectations caused Zabransky to press and lose his edge. Some local sports writers and bloggers wondered if he was overrated and might never recover his 2004 level of play. He consulted with a psychologist before the '06 season, and the coaches went to great pains to figure out ways to reduce his penchant for turnovers (23) in the 2005 season. The best medicine to relieve his anxiety, however, would come in the form of a great running back.

OVERACHIEVERS OR OVERLOOKED?

The University of Nevada media guide for the 2007 matchup with Boise State boasted that the November 25, 2006, game played between the two teams at Mackay Stadium in Reno drew a crowd of 25,506, the tenth largest in stadium history. What the media guide omitted was that 10,000 of those attending had flown or driven the 423 miles from Boise to watch the Broncos, not the Wolf Pack.

Boise State could have choked on that Saturday afternoon in Reno, considering a BCS bowl bid was on the line, but they didn't. Star running back Ian Johnson spent five nights in the dingy dark wing of a San Jose, California, hospital recuperating from a collapsed lung he had received in a hard-fought contest with the San Jose State Spartans two weeks earlier. After sitting out the previous week's game, it was not known how effective he might be against Nevada. Johnson surprised even himself with the most carries in a game all season, thirty-one, with 147 rushing yards and three touchdowns. BSU went on to dominate a good Humanitarian Bowl-bound Nevada football team by a score of 38–7.

Cool Runnings

Ian Johnson was one of several players from the fertile prospecting grounds of Southern California where the Boise State coaches placed much of their recruiting emphasis in the fall of 2003. Johnson, safety Marty Tadman, and offensive tackle Ryan Clady were all recruited within a radius of about seventy-five miles and would form a triumvirate to match or exceed the best BSU players ever at their respective positions. While Tadman was (according to the recruiting services) a three-star prospect, with scholarship offers from three other Pac-10 programs, amazingly, future All-Americans Johnson and Clady were not heavily recruited.

Johnson, from Damien High School in the Los Angles suburb of La Verne, was not judged to be among the top 131 nationally ranked prep running backs by *Scout.com* for the 2004 recruit class, instead being relegated to a group of 140 two-star backs. Ten high school running backs in the state of California were designated as three- and four-stars by *Scout* for the same class, including Marshawn Lynch, future University of California star and number one draft choice in '07 of the Buffalo Bills.

To illustrate how arbitrary rankings and ratings of prospects often are, of all the blue chip running backs from California in that year's recruiting class who were rated ahead of Johnson (with the exception of Lynch), six went on to play Division I football through the 2008 season (one player converted to defense, but only played two years as a back-up). Arian Foster of Mission Bay High School in San Diego is the only player from the top-ten other than Lynch who could be proclaimed successful during his career. Foster compiled a total of 2,964 rushing yards and twenty-three touchdowns in four years for the University of Tennessee.

Discounting Lynch's three-year numbers of 3,230 rushing yards and thirty-five touchdowns, which were below Johnson's totals of 3,406 and forty-six for the same number of seasons, the rest of the California blue chip running backs combined for slightly more than Johnson's total career rushing yards of 4,184 through the 2008 season.

After manhandling Sacramento State in the 2006 season opener, Boise State was matched-up against possibly the best Oregon State team it had played in the fourth and final game of a home and home series that started in 2003. OSU would eventually generate a ten-win season, including a victory over USC and a bowl win over Missouri. Johnson's regular season defining moments came in the home game against OSU when he rushed for 240 yards of his year-end total 1,713 accompanied by a single game team record-tying five of the twenty-five touchdowns he scored in the season with a 42–14 pasting of the Beavers.

Johnson went on to lead the nation in touchdowns, rank fourth in total rushing yards, be named to three All-American squads (first team *Sports Illustrated*, second team *Sporting News*, third team *Associated Press*), and garner an eighth place vote for the Heisman Trophy. He put an exclamation on the 2006 season with the game-winning two-point conversion run in the 2007 Fiesta Bowl, and then proposed to his fiancée on national television during the post-game celebration. Johnson ended his career by eclipsing former San Diego State running back great Marshall Faulk's all-time WAC record for touchdowns with a new standard of fifty-eight in the 2008 Poinsettia Bowl.

My Cousin Vinny

Vinny Perretta is the son of Ralph Perretta, a former stalwart San Diego Chargers center/guard who, from 1975 to 1980, anchored the Chargers' offensive line and helped protect future Hall of Fame quarterback Dan Fouts. Though Vinny came from good football stock, the gene pool got mixed up—his dad was a strapping, (though undersized for an NFL lineman) 6 foot 2, 255 pounds. The chip came off the block at 5 foot 9, 170 pounds as an Encinitas, California, La Costa Canyon High School utility player.

In an all-star football game during the summer of 2004 that included many of the top high school players in San Diego County, San Diego Chargers Pro Bowl linebacker Donnie Edwards was the honorary captain for the game. Edwards raved about the multi-faceted talents of a player who had accepted a scholarship to play at San Diego State that year, sleek 6 foot 2, 195 pound wide receiver, DeMarco Sampson. Though Perretta scored the only touchdown on an eighteen yard pass reception for the north team, he was only mentioned in a postgame article as the son of former Chargers offensive lineman, Ralph Perretta.

With a pocket full of scholarship offers from several other schools, Sampson possessed all of the measurables in abundance and was named by a recruiting service as one of the top three prospects from San Diego County. He became a member of San Diego State's recruit class judged by *Rivals.com* to be the second best (forty-sixth overall) among non-BCS schools for 2004. Perretta, a walk-on with no D-I scholarship offers, was invisible on the recruiting websites as a prospect and became part of Boise State's eighty-fifth ranked class.

Vinny earned his scholarship by playing on the scout team, where he outperformed all of the other scholarship recruits for offensive player of the year honors. He made the two-deep roster his freshman and sophomore years, was a starter for two seasons (a promising junior year as a starter ended with an early-season injury) and a key performer in three bowl games. In addition to punt and kick return duties during his career, he caught seventy-four passes for 991 yards and four touchdowns, rushed for 479 yards on eighty-two carries and six touchdowns, and was 2–2 with two touchdown passes, one of which many consider to be the second most memorable in Bronco football history, in the 2007 Fiesta Bowl against Oklahoma.

DeMarco Sampson, hobbled by injuries for much of his career, finally earned a spot on the two-deep roster in 2008. So far in his time as an Aztec, Sampson has made seventeen pass receptions for 171 yards, seven kick returns for 110 yards, and returned two punts for two yards.

While Vinny's teams were racking up fifty-five wins and playing in five consecutive bowl games, SDSU produced eighteen wins, five losing seasons, and no bowl games (of the ten common opponents during the period, BSU had a 9–1 record to SDSU's 3–7). Most ironic of all occurrences, however, had to be when Vinny and his Broncos were chosen to play in the Poinsettia Bowl in San Diego's Qualcomm Stadium, at the end of his college career in 2008. Qualcomm is the home stadium for San Diego State University.

Walk-ons Rock

Walk-on players who are eventually awarded scholarships are a rarity for Division I football and almost unheard of at the major BCS universities. Even more unusual is a walk-on, non-kicker who earns a scholarship and then makes the two-deep roster for a team. At most Division I programs, one hundred or more players at any given time may make up the total roster, but less than half of those are starters, backups, and special teams players. With a new crop of scholarship players entering the program each year, walk-ons must overcome major obstacles to earn a scholarship and stay in or move up the roster hierarchy.

Vinny Perretta's success story is no aberration in the recruiting history of Boise State, where walk-ons have been the rule rather than the exception. Since 1998, when Dirk Koetter became head coach, and through the fall camp preceding the '09 season, forty-three walk-on players eventually earned a scholarship. In addition, almost every walk-on who has earned a scholarship eventually made the two-deep roster, and most of those became starters. Some, like local high school players tight end Jeb Putzier and running back Brock Forsey, earned all-conference honors and were drafted by NFL teams.

The Sword in the Stone

Brock Forsey embodied the college football walk-on when, in the face of overwhelming odds, he succeeded well beyond what anyone but he thought possible. Forsey was a running back from Centennial High School in the Boise suburb of Meridian. As an all-state selection and the top rusher in his conference, he led Centennial to the state 5A championship his senior year. With unimpressive size/speed measurables, he was not recruited by any Division I programs but was offered the opportunity to walk-on at Boise State.

Forsey blasted into the spotlight with BSU's first appearance in the 1999 Humanitarian Bowl. Seemingly out of nowhere, the redshirt freshman back-up running back tallied a record 269 all-purpose yards, including 152 rushing, to lead Boise State in a dramatic win over Louisville. His offensive MVP performance in the H-Bowl was only the beginning of a career that would place him in a very short roll call of a special class of BSU running backs.

In the first conference game between Boise State and Fresno State at Fresno's Bulldog Stadium in 2001, where a record crowd witnessed BSU's next "biggest game ever," Forsey demonstrated all the qualities that would elevate him to the top of the charts. Behind by a touchdown and extra point, BSU had the ball just inside Fresno State's five-yard line. As the last seconds of the third quarter were expiring, Bronco offensive coordinator Chris Petersen called a sweep to the right side. Forsey grabbed the deep pitch from quarterback Ryan Dinwiddie on about the ten-yard line and scampered toward the end zone. At the four-yard line, as several defensive players formed a four-yard wall to stop him, he propelled himself high into the air, soaring over and through four defenders to score the touchdown. Boise State would record the biggest upset in school history to that point against then unbeaten and number eight-ranked Fresno State.

Forsey went on to make the WAC all-conference first team three years in a row, and was named offensive player of the year for the conference his last season. At the end of his senior year of 2002, he led the nation in scoring with thirty-two touchdowns and gained 1,611 rushing yards. In the spring NFL draft of 2003, Forsey was selected in the sixth round by the Chicago Bears and even started a couple of games during his rookie season. He made a courageous effort in the NFL, but with no deficiency in heart, the lack of size and speed were inadequacies he could not overcome at the next level.

Perhaps the greatest tribute ever bestowed upon him, however, comes from "The Brock Forsey Experience," a Chicago Bears fan organization that still exists today, long after he was cut by the Bears and left as a free agent early in 2004. Each week during the NFL season the group hands out the "Brock Forsey Award" to the Bears player who represents what the group calls "the qualities that the Chicago Bears are known for: toughness, excelling in the absence of great athletic ability, and getting the job done in the face of adversity." That perfectly sums up Brock Forsey.

TALENT IS AS TALENT DOES

From 1988 through 2001, Fresno State generated the fourth best record among all mid-majors at 107–61, won six conference championships, played in eight bowl games, and sent nineteen players to the NFL via the draft. The Bulldogs' list of top picks included first rounders quarterbacks Trent Dilfer in '94 and David Carr in '02. Quarterback Billy Volek, who sandwiched his playing time at Fresno State between Dilfer and Carr, signed as a free-agent in 2000 and is still a back-up for the San Diego Chargers in the 2009 season.

When current head coach Pat Hill started at Fresno State in 1997, he committed to a "play anybody, anytime, anywhere" philosophy that included scheduling as many major college teams as he could during a season. Unfortunately for Hill, most of the major programs either didn't want to play home-and-home schedules or would buy out of previously signed agreements, requiring them to play in Fresno. That meant he had to take his team on the road, often on consecutive Saturdays, to play murderous early season schedules.

Between the years 2000 and 2004, Fresno State played fourteen BCS conference teams to start each season, including Ohio State, UCLA, California, Colorado, Oregon State, Wisconsin, Tennessee, Oklahoma, Washington, and Kansas State. Only three of those games were at Fresno's Bulldog Stadium (Oregon State twice, and Cal). Even with a grueling schedule that sometimes required his team to fly across the Rocky Mountains twice within a three-week span, Hill compiled a very respectable 7–7 record against his major college opponents.

In 1999, June Jones decided to accept what appeared to be the impossible task of turning around what had become a mediocre program at the University of Hawaii. During the 1998 season, Jones became the interim head coach for the San Diego Chargers and was offered the permanent position for the following year. Instead, he went to Honolulu and immediately turned the Warriors into a mainstay in the Western Athletic Conference. Jones produced the greatest reversal in college football history when he transformed a 0–12 team in 1998 into a 9–4 team with a win over Oregon State in a bowl game one year later. Before leaving Hawaii at the end of the 2007 season, Jones became the most successful coach in the island school's history with a record of 75–41.

From the seasons of 2002 through 2009, more than 90 percent of Fresno State's recruits were homegrown Californians and over 40 percent of those came from the Central Valley. Hawaii signed nearly 80 percent of its scholarship players from the two states of California and Hawaii, while almost 40 percent of that group originated in the islands. Only 14 percent of Boise State's recruits could call Idaho home, while nearly half came from California and the other 38 percent were scattered among sixteen states and Canada.

For the ten seasons from 1999 through 2008, Hawaii produced the fourth best winning percentage and Fresno State the sixth best of all mid-major programs. Fresno State went to nine bowl games, while Hawaii played in seven. Boise State employed three different head coaches for the ten-year period, whereas Fresno State maintained the same coach, and Hawaii didn't make a coaching change until 2008. Since 2001, when Boise State joined the WAC, and through 2008, the Broncos won six of the eight conference championships, while Hawaii won one (2007) and Fresno State none. As successful as these two programs have been, they generated a combined record against Boise State of 2–14 (one win each) in eight consecutive seasons of WAC competition.

Just the Facts

For the ten seasons starting in 1999 and ending in 2008, Boise State recorded eight of ten seasons with seven or more consecutive wins, had seven consecutive seasons with seven or more consecutive wins (second only to Michigan in the modern football era), and a total of twenty losses. TCU, with the second best winning percentage of all mid-majors during the period, totaled twelve more losses than BSU and recorded a pair of consecutive seasons with seven or more consecutive wins. Only three non-BCS conference schools, Boise State, TCU, and Utah, were among the top twenty-five winningest FBS programs, and second place among the smaller schools, TCU, was separated from BSU by nine BCS conference teams.

Many factors can affect win-loss records for teams over a ten-year period, but one may conclude that, apart from poor coaching, an inability to draw consistently significant numbers of blue chip recruits every year, along with dependence on player development, makes it extremely difficult for even the best of the mid-majors to maintain the same level of winning consistency as the best BCS teams.

After a closer study of season-to-season records from 1999 through 2008, a strong case can be made that much of the short-term success experienced by most non-BCS programs during that period can be attributed to the presence of an NFL-caliber, dominant offensive skill player. For example, quarterbacks Chad Pennington and Byron Leftwich of Marshall, David Carr of Fresno State, Ben Roethlisberger of

Miami of Ohio, Alex Smith of Utah, David Garrard of East Carolina, and running backs LaDainian Tomlinson of TCU and Chris Johnson of East Carolina, all led their respective mid-major teams to unprecedented success and national prominence.

Each school was able to match or exceed its best season or series of seasons ever and in several instances score impressive wins over BCS teams with these standout players, seven of whom would become NFL first round draft choices and all eventually earned status as starters (Garrard was a 4th round pick). However, the same programs had inconsistent, average, or even poor records before or after the presence of these players.

In the five seasons before Tomlinson started playing at TCU, the Horned Frogs produced two winning seasons and a 24–32 record. During Tomlinson's sophomore through senior years of play they were 25–11, and in his senior year of 2000 the 10–2 record was by far the best for TCU in more than a half century. Through 2008, Marshall cannot boast of a winning season since '03, though Pennington's 13–0 team in 1999 is the best ever for that school and Leftwich's teams produced a 30–9 record from '00 through '02. Even Miami, the team Roethlisberger took to 13–1 in '03 and unquestionably its best in history, lost ten games in one season only three years later. In the year prior to Alex Smith's first season as a starter, Utah lost six games, and only one year after the Utes' spectacular undefeated Fiesta Bowl season of 2004, they were an unspectacular 7–5.

East Carolina enjoyed a three-year run of 23–13 and triumphs over eight BCS teams with Garrard at the helm, including a win over Texas Tech in the GalleryFurniture.com Bowl in 2000. After his departure for the NFL at the end of the '01 season starting in 2002 and through 2005, ECU dropped to a 12–34 record and four consecutive losing seasons before being rescued by Chris Johnson in '06 and '07 (two winning seasons with a combined record of 15–11).

In 2008, Ball State University produced a twelve-win undefeated regular season and Division I national rankings; both firsts in school history. The Cardinals' success brought an attempt by the WAC's Humanitarian Bowl to match them against undefeated Boise State in a season ending bowl game. The matchup never materialized and Ball State went on to lose the Mid-American Conference championship game to Buffalo, followed by a season-ending bowl loss.

Ball State is to be commended for an outstanding season, but much of their success originated with the excellent throwing arm of 6 foot 2, 217-pound quarterback Nate Davis. Starting in 1999 with an 0–11 season, Ball State did not produce a winning record (ranked ninety-ninth of 120 D-I teams through 2007) until Davis's first season as a full-time starter in 2007. At the end of his junior year of '08, Davis decided to forgo his final year of eligibility and declared for the NFL draft. He was taken by the San Francisco 49ers in the fifth round, where he earned a roster spot as the number three quarterback for the 2009 season.

Since 1999, Boise State has averaged nearly eleven wins per season, but suffered only minor deviations and less than ten wins in only two years ('01 with eight wins and '05 with nine wins). The team with the second best mid-major winning percentage, TCU, won only six games the year after Tomlinson left for the NFL. Three years later, in 2003, with the first eleven-win season in fifty-three years, the Horned Frogs lost to Boise State in the Fort Worth Bowl, then the following year had a losing record and won only five games.

Boise State ended 2004 with a 12–1 record and a final AP poll ranking of number twelve with the second youngest team in the FBS, a quarterback in his first year as a starter, seven starters or key backups who were former walk-ons, and not a single player was drafted by an NFL team in '05. By contrast, Oregon State, winner over Notre Dame in the Insight.com Bowl and whom BSU beat handily in a game during the regular season, had a veteran team with three draftees, including 2008 Pro Bowl quarterback Derek Anderson. BYU, another Bronco victim, also had three players drafted. Fresno State, with a 9–3 season, national rankings in two polls at number twenty-two and a Humanitarian Bowl win over Virginia, was manhandled by Boise State in conference play, yet could boast a number one and number four round draft pick, both of whom were starters for New England's 2008 Super Bowl team. Louisville, with arguably its best team in history through the 2004 season and six players drafted, beat BSU in the Liberty Bowl, but the game was a furious back and forth battle with the outcome in doubt until the final seconds.

From 2004 through 2008, the Broncos won four of five conference championships, yet the first team all-conference quarterback was from somewhere other than Boise State every year. After BSU's 2006 undefeated Fiesta Bowl winning season, Hawaii heralded the WAC offensive player of the year in future NFL draftee Colt Brennan and eleven all-conference players to Boise State's five; to add insult to injury, the Warriors' head coach, June Jones, with a loss to Boise State, was named WAC coach of the year over Chris Petersen.

After dominating the WAC in 2008, no Bronco players were drafted by an NFL team and none of the players signing as free agents made an opening day roster. San Jose State named three draft picks; two second round and one sixth. Hawaii three picks; second, third and sixth. Fresno State two; both in the sixth. Nevada and Idaho sent one each to the NFL by the draft, both in the seventh round. Oregon, who was defeated by Boise State at Eugene during the regular season, had six NFL-drafted players. TCU, with a veteran-laden team, and winner by one point over the Broncos in the Poinsettia Bowl, sent five players to the NFL via the draft.

During Boise State's ten-year reign as a mid-major power, the program has yet to produce an NFL-drafted quarterback, and only one wide receiver in the fifth round (through the 2009 draft). The highest draft pick in the other offensive skill position, running back, occurred in the sixth round. Among drafted players the Broncos can count three tight ends, sixth and seventh rounds; one fullback, sixth round; three offensive linemen, first, second, and fifth rounds; and two defensive backs, second and seventh rounds. Other than Ryan Clady, who had an excellent 2008 rookie season at left tackle with the Denver Broncos, none of the former BSU players can be considered impact players in the NFL.

College football analysts agree it has taken keen perception on the part of the coaching staff to identify and recruit so many quality prospects that other FBS schools have overlooked. *Rivals.com* analyst Jeremy Crabtree said, "I marvel at the job that Boise State does with their evaluations. Broncos coaches find prospects who just end up being great players three years later; that staff projects as well as any in the nation."

In 2006 Boise State could not have produced an undefeated football team that dominated a ten-win, USC-beating, bowl game-winning Oregon State team, then battled toe-to-toe with eleven-game winning, Big 12 champion Oklahoma, without some very good players on the field.

Several players from the Fiesta Bowl winning squad stated that by game day, Coach Petersen had them convinced they were Goliath and Oklahoma was David. A comparison of players drafted from each team in the 2007 draft, and their subsequent success in the NFL, may reveal some truth to the coach's assertion. With the exception of the supremely talented Adrian Peterson, the number one pick of the Minnesota Vikings, who would go on to become 2007 rookie of the year, and St. Louis Rams defensive end

C.J. Ah You, no other players drafted from the 2006 Sooner team in the 2007 draft were listed on an NFL active roster at the beginning of the 2008 season. By comparison, Boise State could identify three of four drafted players who were listed as starters for their respective teams at the beginning of the 2008 NFL season (Korey Hall, Packers; Derrick Schouman, Bills; Gerald Alexander, Lions), and the other player (Legedu Naanee, Chargers), who was listed as a backup wide receiver and special teams player.

The trick plays in the Fiesta Bowl game may have been the topic of discussion by the national media, but it was the players, not the system or the coaches, who executed them to perfection. It should not be overlooked that BSU enjoyed a comfortable eighteen-point lead toward the end of the third quarter when a fluke play gave Oklahoma a gift turnover at the BSU eleven-yard line. ESPN's Pat Forde commented, "Boise State dominated the first forty minutes, making it clear the Western Athletic Conference champion deserved a BCS berth."

Maybe the biggest tribute to the success of the program and the perceived quality of the players and coaching prior to 2009, came in the pre-season of 2007, when the largest weekly sports publication in the country saw fit to include a rebuilding Boise State, decimated by the loss of fourteen key players, as the only non-BCS team in its 2007 preseason top-twenty at number fifteen. Further honor was bestowed on BSU in the week before the early season matchup with the University of Washington, when the odds makers favored the visiting Broncos.

In 1991, when athletic director Gene Bleymaier first began formulating a plan to move Boise State to Division I, the Broncos would lose for the tenth consecutive season to the University of Idaho and were playing a schedule that included Liberty University, Stephen F. Austin, and two-win Cal State Long Beach in its last year of football. In the same year, the University of Washington was winning a second consecutive Rose Bowl game along with a national championship. In 2001, when Boise State joined the Western Athletic Conference after only five years of D-I participation, Washington was winning another Rose Bowl and a number three national ranking.

Had the consummate fan fallen into a coma in 1999 and awakened on the week prior to the BSU-Washington game to be told that the Broncos were owners of the best winning percentage in the FBS since '99, winners over Oklahoma in a major New Year's Day bowl game, awarded a season-ending number five ranking in a major national poll, and now favored to beat the Huskies, he may well have sunk back into an unconscious state from the shock. Even after the game ended in defeat for the Broncos, the headlines seemed amiss when all the major news wires referred to Washington's triumph as an upset.

A solid '07 BSU team produced a ten-win regular season and a top twenty-five national ranking, headed into their bowl matchup with East Carolina University. Ironically, ECU, a school with 6,000 more students, a campus stadium with 12,000 greater seating capacity, a four-year football tradition thirty-seven years longer and Division I participation thirty years earlier than Boise State, "upset" the Broncos with a last minute comeback in the Hawaii Bowl. ECU also fit the mold of a mid-major whose success, at least in part, was due to the presence of a dominant skill player, running back Chris Johnson, an eventual first round NFL draft pick and 2008 rookie of the year runner-up.

The Incredible Hulk

The large majority of football players who have the size and skills to play at the next level are recruited by colleges to play the position they occupied in high school. Occasionally coaches will switch players, or even recruit them for another position, but they are almost always relocated to a position commensurate with their size and measurables from high school—offensive line to defensive line, safety to cornerback, fullback to tight end, etc.

Ryan Winterswyk was a Southern California product from the Los Angeles suburb of La Habra. In high school he was a multi-position player, alternating as a tight end and wide receiver on offense and safety on defense. He had good size at 6 foot 4, 225 pounds, but his speed at defensive back or the receiver positions was not considered D-I quality.

Ryan graduated from high school in the spring of 2005 but didn't receive any college scholarship offers to play football. Armed with an endorsement from his high school coach, he approached Boise State in the fall of 2005 and convinced the coaching staff to give him a walk-on opportunity in the winter semester of 2006. During the spring practice of that year, just as coaches surmised, Winterswyk was a 'tweener, not big enough for the defensive line and not fast enough for linebacker or defensive back.

What the coaches did observe was athleticism, a large frame and the possibility that he could bulk up and play defensive end, so they allowed him to keep his walk-on status in the fall of 2006 and gave him a redshirt. That was all the motivation Ryan needed to get serious in the weight room.

By the spring of 2007, the transformation of Ryan Winterswyk had begun in earnest. With nearly thirty-five weight-room-added pounds, he now looked the part of a defensive lineman. Almost from the first moment he lined up at the defensive end position, the coaches were amazed at his quickness, agility, and strength. Without hesitation they offered him a scholarship.

By mid-season 2007, redshirt freshman Winterswyk established himself as the number three defensive end and played mostly in passing situations to take advantage of his speed. By season's end he led the defensive line in tackles for loss and was honored by a vote of his teammates as the team's top defensive lineman. At the end of the 2008 season, he was voted by his teammates as the co-most valuable defensive player and named first team All-WAC.

WHAT'S THE FORMULA?

Some suggest that Boise State has produced teams comparable to those of the Western Athletic Conference BYU dynasty of the seventies and eighties. After closer scrutiny of both programs, placed in the context of their times, the comparison is not a good one. With a church affiliation like Notre Dame, BYU has always had a national recruiting footprint, able to attract large numbers of blue chip and even a few elite players from every corner of the country. Household names like quarterbacks Jim McMahon and Steve

Young, along with tight end Todd Christensen, were players who not only dominated in college but also went on to produce stellar NFL careers.

From A to BSU

If Boise State is unable to point to tradition, higher rated recruits, NFL caliber impact players, more lavish facilities, larger fan/alumni base, or bigger budget than even some of its conference cohorts, to what do the Broncos owe their eleven-year run of hyper-winning.

One caller to a national sports radio talk show expressed his admiration for Boise State and the program's success by offering, "If there was ever a college football program that could be defined as the whole being vastly greater than the sum of its parts, it's Boise State." In today's modern corporate vernacular, the phrase might be expressed as "somehow the players, coaches, administrators, alumni and community have applied synergy to reach critical mass."

A host of variables factor into the Boise State equation for winning, but Gene Bleymaier's long tenure as Athletic Director and the succession of head coaches since 1998 are a good place to begin. In an era when rapid turnover is the rule, Bleymaier's twenty-eight years at the helm of a major university's athletic department (through 2009) places him in the Methuselah range for time served.

The pressures that accompany the athletic director position at a mid-major university today don't mesh with the phrase "long term commitment." Balancing budgets, meeting Title IX requirements and keeping good coaches in place for a wide variety of sports that also maintain winning records, are only a few of the challenges. A younger, less experienced administrator may have panicked or compromised his normal patterns of due diligence when he was faced with the daunting task of replacing four head football coaches in only ten seasons between 1996 and 2005 as Bleymaier was.

Bleymaier and former BSU president John Keiser worked well together in the late eighties and early nineties, sharing a vision for BSU football. Bleymaier worked tirelessly to find quality coaches and then went to bat for them with the state of Idaho to provide competitive salaries. When Bob Kustra became president of the university in 2003, Bleymaier again was able to solicit a solid commitment from his new boss for a continuance of resources and assistance in identifying, hiring, and keeping the best coaches available.

After Dirk Koetter left for the Arizona State head coaching position at the end of the 2000 season, rather than go outside to hire a new coach from another program, Bleymaier placed greater value on keeping the system relatively status quo by hiring the previous assistant head coach Dan Hawkins.

When Hawkins departed for the Colorado head coaching position at the end of the 2005 season, after all but guaranteeing he would stay, Kustra and Bleymaier agreed that Petersen was the best fit as his replacement. Petersen demonstrated that he could produce one of the most dynamic offenses in college football and, just as important, had gained the full trust of his players. Hawkins owned a combined 9–1 record against Pat Hill's Fresno State and June Jones's Hawaii during his tenure, but even with a new contract signed after the '04 season, he was still earning substantially less than either of those coaches.

Both administrators knew they would be required to make an offer to Petersen that was unprecedented in terms of its total compensation for a Boise State head coach. The commitment was made, Petersen accepted a five-year, $4.25 million contract with incentives, and he became the highest paid employee of the state of Idaho.

The Three Amigos

In 1998 head coach Dirk Koetter, the son of a high school coach and a Pocatello, Idaho native, developed the first of a series of teams that would produce eleven consecutive winning seasons and the best winning percentage in the FBS since then. His offensive philosophy, which was adopted in principle by successor coaches Dan Hawkins and Chris Petersen, has allowed Boise State to create the highest average points per game total in the FBS since 1999.

Before being called to his first head coaching position at Boise State, Koetter was as pure an offensive football coach as any in the country. His first full-time coaching job was as offensive coordinator at San Francisco State in 1985, followed by stints in the same capacity at UTEP, Missouri, and Boston College, before relocating back to the West with a two-year stop at the University of Oregon.

At Boise State, Koetter was a technician who rarely stepped out of his coaching role into that of community organizer. His work ethic and loyalty were never questioned, but it was suggested by some that he was not comfortable with the media/booster side of the coaching business.

Not surprisingly, he almost exclusively managed the offense and called the plays. He was considerably more animated on the sidelines and in the locker room than either of the relatively mild-mannered Hawkins or Petersen; once he even threw a chair, shattering it against the wall during halftime.

Hawkins, who was Koetter's first assistant coach selection at BSU, reflected a more varied background. He coached first at his alma mater, UC Davis, then spent two years as a head coach in the high school ranks and five years as a community college assistant coach before accepting his first college head coaching position at Oregon's Willamette University in 1993. Hawkins appeared well on his way to creating a small college dynasty at Willamette, working his way to 40 wins and a 13–1 1997 season, including a berth in the NAIA finals.

Under Koetter, Hawkins was assistant head coach and tight ends/special teams coach. During his three years as the top assistant, he honed his already sharp management skills, which dovetailed perfectly with his elevation to head coach in 2001. As head coach he proved to be an excellent manager, possessing an innate ability to recruit good coaches and delegate responsibility.

Hawkins was much more the philosopher/motivator than either Koetter or Petersen. Former Boise State Bronco and current Philadelphia Eagles All-Pro safety Quintin Mikell credited Hawkins with being able to convince the players they could beat anybody. Some members of the local media thought him too close to the vest with player issues, and one local pundit went so far as to comment that he felt like a puppy dog following Hawkins around, waiting for an occasional bone, but never getting the full meal.

Petersen was an undersized quarterback at UC Davis, where he captured the Northern California Athletic Conference Player of the Year award and was the top-rated Division II quarterback in the nation at the end of his senior year. After playing under young assistant coach Dan Hawkins, he spawned his offensive pedigree at his alma mater, as the receivers coach for five years after graduation. He followed that with a one-year stay at Pitt as quarterbacks coach and another short two years at Portland State as quarterbacks coach before joining the Oregon staff in 1993, where he served as the receivers coach until joining Hawkins in 2001.

Petersen's star rose quickly when, after the 2001 season, he received offers from three BCS programs to serve as offensive coordinator. He elected to stay in Boise, turning down what would have been potentially more money and seemingly greater opportunity. For the next four seasons, Petersen's offenses continued to produce some of the highest scoring averages in the FBS.

Petersen enjoyed his tenure as offensive coordinator and for five seasons admitted that he preferred the play-calling isolation of the booth to the sidelines. He did not feel a natural calling to be the head coach, and only accepted the position after much soul searching. It was thought by some of the local media that he was a technician with too great a focus on detail to be successful as a head coach. After three years, he has proven his critics wrong with the best record of any FBS head coach over that period. Petersen consistently maintains a warm, unassuming demeanor when facing the public, but the youthful good looks and understatements to the press belie his steadfastness to a creed that is bent on winning every game.

College coaches don't just stumble upon coaching jobs; they typically acquire new positions as the result of prior partnerships often going back many years. In the case of Petersen and Hawkins both were players and assistant coaches under Jim Sochor, the College Football Hall of Fame head coach for the University of California, Davis from 1970 to 1988.

A previously dismal UC Davis football program which had not fielded a winning team in twenty-two seasons, was transformed into a Division II dynasty under Sochor. He won eighteen consecutive league championships, more than any other football program at any level in NCAA history, and posted a 156–42–5 record. Sochor's accomplishments are even more remarkable, considering he was forced to operate with some of the most austere practice, training and stadium facilities in any division of college football.

Sochor was as comfortable championing the philosophies of Chopra and Taoism to gain the respect of his players as he was drawing Xs and Os on the chalkboard. His practice sessions often resembled a corporate retreat for senior executives with exercises in team-building, emphasizing the values of trust and unity. He reminded his players that almost every team they played against had bigger, faster, and more athletic players than UC Davis, so the only way to compete was to play as a cohesive unit not as a group of individuals.

Former University of Oregon head coach Mike Belotti, the most successful in that school's history, also played for and coached under Sochor from 1970 to 1976. Though Koetter did not attend UC Davis, he was offensive coordinator for a San Francisco State team humbled by Sochor's Aggies 65–12 in 1985, and later worked for Belotti as his offensive coordinator at Oregon.

When Hawkins and Petersen began their quest in 2001 to build on the success created by Koetter, they found themselves in a somewhat similar environment as that experienced by their former mentor over three decades earlier. Boise State was by no means in the same dire condition as perennial loser Cal Davis had been at the time of Sochor's takeover, but the overall facilities were limited and in disrepair, and the community needed a champion for the program to assure them that the Broncos could compete in the new conference.

It was not encouraging that, according to the "experts" who ranked prospects in the late 90s and early 2000s, the quality of the recruits coming into the program was only average at best, compared to other teams in the WAC. Both coaches discovered early on that their recruiting work was cut out for them; blue chips were not an option and the recruiting trail would run well beyond the confines of the Northwest.

As Hawkins began imparting his philosophy to the players, he also set in motion the hard work of selling the program to the alumni and fan base and rallying support to improve the facilities. The legwork and effort he put into eliciting administration, community and alumni support was like nothing ever seen before in a Boise State head football coach. It seemed he spent as much time meeting with community groups and giving presentations, as he did walking the sidelines.

Though Hawkins is on record for having given credit to Koetter for setting the tone and giving the program the boost it needed to be successful at the Division I level, it is Hawkins who made the school administration, faculty leadership, students, community and the players believe they could do everything he said they could. There was no inherent reason for Boise State to excel above and beyond the other members of the new and evolving WAC, except that Hawkins believed they could.

When Hawkins left for Colorado at the end of the 2005 season, Petersen was unanimously received by the players as the best possible replacement. Petersen is no less ubiquitous in the community today than was

Hawkins, but as would be expected, their methods contrast. The Hawkins one-liners and quotes from any number of philosophers have been replaced by Petersen's laid-back, more open-dialoged approach.

Has the Hawkins/Petersen flavor of the Sochor philosophy that operates contrary to many traditional coaching principles, been effective at Boise State? It appears after eight years under one or both coaches, that it may be at the top of the list of reasons the Broncos have excelled well beyond other conference members.

In the final analysis, Gene Bleymaier's thought process and good fortune that led him to hire this trio of coaches with like mind and talent is one of many blessings he must count every day. Management personnel turnover due to poor choices by superiors has derailed more successful organizations than anyone can guess. For Boise State it appears that the seamless nature of Bleymaier's strategy to maintain relative consistency in coaching philosophy must be counted as a key contributor to Bronco football's sustained success since 2001.

The Terminator

With the average career length for a player in the NFL lasting only three and a half years, very few are fortunate enough to play in a Super Bowl and also be selected to the All-Pro team. What's more, the roll call for this elite group rarely includes players who were un-drafted free-agents after college.

Boise State safety Quintin Mikell was not drafted by a single NFL team in the spring of 2003. Instead, he signed with the Philadelphia Eagles as a free agent after forty-seven defensive backs were selected in the draft. Mikell made his presence known early by becoming a special teams ace in his first year and in 2005 and 2006 was named the special teams MVP for the Eagles. In 2007, he signed a four-year contract and became a starter at strong safety. In 2008, he was honored with a second team NFL All-Pro selection.

Mikell was a multi-sport athlete from Willamette High School in Eugene, Oregon. On the football field he was a dynamo, playing multiple positions, but preferring defense, where he was a ferocious tackler. He was a fine all-around athlete, but at 5 foot 10, 170 pounds, there didn't appear to be a sport he had the size and skill to play at the college level.

Neither of the Oregon Pac-10 schools, including the University of Oregon in his hometown, seemed to believe he had the size and speed to succeed in the defensive secondary, so no football scholarships were offered. Dirk Koetter was just beginning his new job as BSU head coach at the end of 1997 when he received a tip about Mikell from a former Oregon Duck football player. Koetter saw a tenacity and athleticism that transcended his size and tendered an offer to Mikell.

At Boise State, Mikell earned his stripes as a scout team member in his redshirt season. During spring practice he began to show flashes of what was to be a brilliant Bronco football career. Before the first game of the 1999 season, he was named a starter at the safety position.

From 1999 through 2002 Mikell's four teams won forty games, including a victory over previously unbeaten and number eight ranked Fresno State and finished three seasons with bowl wins. He was the conference defensive player of the year in 2000 (Big West) and again in 2002 (WAC). After being named team captain his senior year, he ended his career with 401 tackles, good for second place all-time in the Bronco record book.

A PHILOSOPHY FOR WINNING

Before San Jose State's home game against Boise State during the 2008 season, Spartans' head coach Dick Tomey pronounced his team to be the best he had produced in his four-year tenure. Tomey, with his recent addition of a handful of blue chip transfers from Pac-10 programs, along with a freakishly big and fast group of defensive linemen and linebackers, including Western Athletic Conference Defensive Player of the Year Jarron Gilbert, appeared to offer the Broncos what some considered its stiffest competition in the WAC.

It was mid-season and Boise State was climbing the national polls with a six-game win streak, but looked vulnerable to a letdown. San Jose State, with its best start to a season since joining the WAC in 2001, seemed poised to spring an upset. The game was hyped locally, and the largest home crowd of the season was prepared to will its team to victory.

San Jose State had never beaten Boise State in eight tries (seven WAC games and a non-WAC loss dating back to 1978), and a number of elements seemed to favor the Spartans. The biggest advantage, however, may have been Tomey's highly acclaimed defensive mind. If anyone could exploit a young freshman quarterback and an undersized, inexperienced offensive line, it was the man whose superb defenses at the University of Arizona earned the moniker "Desert Swarm" in the late 80s and early 90s.

The Bronco Nation recalled BSU's last two visits to San Jose, when the Broncos escaped with an overtime win in 2004 and a game ending field goal to break a tie in 2006, allowing them to preserve undefeated regular seasons. If the motivation to end a seven-game conference losing streak and vengeance to amend for those two heartbreaking home field losses didn't inspire the San Jose State players, the law of averages had to catch up with Boise State sometime.

What the Spartan contingent forgot, but had to be abruptly reminded of by ESPN color commentator Rod Gilmore during the game was, "Boise State wins the games it is supposed to win." With a dominating defense that held the San Jose State offense to nine first downs, and a methodical offense that rolled up twenty-eight first downs, the Broncos walked away from Spartan Stadium with a relatively easy 33–16 win.

X's and O's

The current Boise State offense, which has been altered only slightly since 2001, might best be described as a blend of styles. Many who are aware of the Broncos' prolific scoring offenses over the past ten years are unaware that the "spread", utilized by the majority of college teams today, is not the staple scheme. Instead, Petersen relies on multiple shifts that may spread out on one play, contrasted with a two-back power running scheme on the next.

In his quest to maximize performance and find an edge that separates his teams from those of the other conference members, Coach Pete has taken a page from the old single wing offensive playbook of Lyle Smith's Boise Junior College teams and its direct-snap-receiving tailback. In the last three years, he has introduced the occasional use of an athletic utility player who can take direct snaps from center and utilize his athleticism to run or throw the ball. The strategy relies on the hopes of creating both mismatches and surprise. Variations of the formation allow the player to pass/run option, hand off, or throw the ball back to the quarterback.

As much as the continuity of offensive philosophy has been vital in maintaining consistency, it is also apparent that each of the three coaches since 1998 shares the same ability to develop players to fit his schemes. Without prototype dominant athletes, they have been able to systemize quarterbacks, wide receivers and tight ends, and then exploit their strengths to the fullest. With undersized and less-athletic players on defense, the coaches have stressed discipline in maintaining their zones of play on the field. One coach affirmed, "We may be outsized in many match-ups, but we will not allow ourselves to be outsmarted."

All three coaches concur that a highly skilled quarterback is essential to the success of their offense, but Bart Hendricks, Ryan Dinwiddie, and Jared Zabransky were not blessed with the combination of physical stature, athletic prowess and/or throwing arms possessed by the likes of future NFL players Chris Redman from Louisville, David Carr from Fresno State, Seneca Wallace from Iowa State, or Derek Anderson and Matt Moore, both from Oregon State. However, on five occasions a Boise State quarterback matched or outperformed his counterpart and was able to direct convincing wins over the teams led by these players.

By the end of the 2001 season, it was apparent that Dinwiddie owned all of the skills to be an outstanding college quarterback. In 2002 with the junior signal-caller at the helm, Boise State was poised to take over the WAC with a solid veteran squad. In the second game of the season at Arkansas the quarterback fractured his leg in the first half. It appeared to many after the 41–14 shellacking at the hands of the Razorbacks that BSU's promising season was about to go down in flames.

Seemingly proving the point that the system is at least partially responsible for Boise State's unusual success, senior career back-up quarterback B. J. Rhode took over the reins and led the Broncos to four dominating victories in a row, including a 58–31 win over eventual WAC runner-up and 10-game winner Hawaii. Dinwiddie returned to humiliate year-end bowl-game winning Fresno State 67–21, and direct the Broncos to an unblemished record through the remainder of the season, including a Humanitarian Bowl win over Iowa State.

Though mid-majors have shown themselves to be vulnerable to greater volatility with respect to their win-loss records, Boise State bucks the trend over the past ten years. The '01, '04, '07, and '08 seasons brought into focus the exceptional skill of Hawkins and Petersen to build highly successful teams in major transition years. In all four of those seasons, a new and untested quarterback replaced a starter. Each year presented coaches with unique challenges—'01 with a significant upgrade in competition entering a new conference, '04 with the second youngest group of starters in D-1, '07 with the loss of every starting receiver and one backup, and '08 the loss of four of the most productive offensive linemen in Boise State history.

In 2007, Petersen's choice for starting quarterback was a fifth year senior who had never started a game and played mostly in mop-up situations. Taylor Tharp was not even the expected winner of the battle for the starting position at the beginning of fall camp. The coaching staff, however, found a way to mold a highly coachable player into a very successful pocket passer with statistics, including a completion ratio of 68 percent, 3,340 passing yards and thirty touchdowns, placing him among the elite quarterbacks in the country. All of Tharp's receivers were new starters, and two true freshmen generated more than 50 percent of the wide receiver touchdowns and nearly the same percentage of the yardage.

2008 brought another attention-grabbing battle for starting quarterback. A fifth-year senior with strong athletic ability, but never a starter, and a third-year sophomore with prototypical size and a strong arm, competed with a redshirt freshman. Petersen decided on Kellen Moore over Bush Hamden and Michael Coughlin, and for the first time in Bronco history a redshirt freshman opened the season at quarterback. An instant success, Moore ended the 2008 campaign ranked twelfth nationally in quarterback efficiency.

When Boise State opened the 2008 season, nobody questioned the depth and talent positioned at wide receiver and running back. However, a redshirt freshman quarterback, one of the smallest if not the most inexperienced offensive lines in the conference, inconsistent play by the linebackers in '07 and a lightly regarded group of defensive tackles, did not appear to be a formula for hyper-success. The bar was raised so high by teams of the previous nine years and expectations were such that the 2008 version apparently could do nothing else but meet the standard. The Broncos reloaded and blasted through a third undefeated regular season in five years (12–0), an eighth conference championship in ten years and a ninth bowl appearance since 1999.

Each coach was fully aware that he would never be able to attract highly rated prospects, but no matter a player's ranking, an emphasis has always been placed on character and work ethic in the prospect selection process. "In Boise, Idaho, you can't just win, you've got to do it with class, integrity, and character," said recruiting coordinator Viliami Tuivai to a reporter at Scout.com. "Wherever you go here, people know you play for Boise State. We aren't going to recruit a bunch of kids that'll rampage through our community. We want them to have a positive effect in every way."

Petersen has expressed on several occasions that he recruits players who are true student athletes. Demonstrating that the "proof is in the pudding", Boise State has ranked in the upper percentile of every FBS [3]Academic Progress Rate (APR), since the NCAA introduced the reform to increase academic standards for athletes in 2005. In the spring of 2009 the program attained a 966 rating that was behind only Stanford and Air Force Academy of the twenty-six major college football programs in the West.

---

3 The Academic Progress Rate (also known as APR) is a metric established by the NCAA to measure the success or failure of collegiate athletic teams in moving student-athletes toward graduation. It was instituted in February of 2005. Collegiate sports teams that fail to achieve an APR score of 925 - equivalent to a 50 percent graduation rate - may be penalized with the loss of scholarships. A perfect score is 1000. The APR is calculated by allocating points for eligibility and retention—the two factors that research identifies as the best indicators of graduation. Each player on a given roster earns a maximum of two points per term, one for being academically eligible and one for staying with the institution. A team's APR is the total points of a team's roster at a given time divided by the total points possible.

Tony Altieri believes that head coaches Koetter, Hawkins and Petersen were/are uniquely aligned in the way they view prospects. Coaches today recognize that there is much more of a "what's in it for me attitude" by many high school football players with FBS talent. Players often become enamored by the attention they receive as a result of the recruiting process and take that attitude into their college playing careers.

In thirteen years of Division I play the Boise State coaches have never been in a position to recruit more than the occasional four-star player, but any high school prospect who makes the jump to Boise State is elite in his league, town, city, county, or, in the case of Idaho, state.

Many players commit to a program with the belief they are so uniquely skilled that their mere presence will make the team better. Altieri thinks that the three coaches were/are able to sense if a recruit is of the self-focused variety that sees himself as a unique star, and so they steer clear.

Petersen takes a cue from his former college coach/mentor, Sochor, and maintains that there are no special status players on his teams, though he is very complimentary of superior individual game and practice performances. He also never dwells on a single player during press conferences as being significantly more important to winning than the team as a whole. In 2007, when he sensed that players were becoming preoccupied with their individual importance over that of the team, he had their names removed from the back of the jerseys. The message rang loud and clear, and order was restored to the blue-collar work ethic.

With an average of almost four starters or key back-ups per year having been former non-scholarship recruits, no FBS program in the country has been more dependent on walk-ons than Boise State over the past ten years. The Broncos have relied heavily on their ability to find players like former defensive tackle Andrew Browning, a member of the 2006 undefeated Fiesta Bowl winning team. Browning was not recruited by any FBS programs and wasn't even recruited by the Broncos to be a walk-on. Instead, he was forced to send a letter and video tape to ask for a tryout seeking to qualify as a non-scholarship player. Browning eventually became a three-year starter, a first team all-conference player in his senior year of 2006, and was twice voted by his teammates as the best defensive lineman at the end of a season.

Hawkins and Petersen recognized that quality player depth is a problem for all mid-major programs, and thus the loss of even two or three key players during a season could result in a losing streak. Their answer has been, in part, to create opportunities for younger back-up players, who are promising but underdeveloped, to substitute for starters more liberally throughout a game. Several players have commented after graduation that it was an opportunity to play in games as a freshman or sophomore that put them to the test, helping them grow in confidence and prepare for the future.

An overlooked aspect of the coaching style of Petersen is his mild manner on the sidelines during both games and practice sessions. He is not prone to outbursts, nor does he typically show overt emotion even in the most negative or positive game situations. This reflects on the players and other coaches, who are businesslike and possibly less likely to allow emotions to overwhelm them in tight game situations.

Humility is not a trait identified with most head football coaches for major college programs, but both Hawkins and Petersen have never been interested in boasting about the program, or overselling it. For example, each has been undisturbed with the BCS controversy swirling around them in recent years. Hawkins, with an undefeated team in the 2004 regular season, didn't try to lobby or complain about the system that didn't allow the Broncos into a BCS bowl game, but instead responded to an L.A. Times reporter in '04, "If the country thinks we're great and awesome, OK; if they think we stink, I'm not going to spend a bunch of time stewing over that."

Petersen likewise wants no part of the BCS debate. When the media asked for his response to the Fiesta Bowl Committee's decision not to give his Bronco team an opportunity to play in the big money bowl game after an undefeated 2008 regular season, he graciously deferred all questions to the "powers that be," or philosophically affirmed, "We can't change the system nor do we have any desire to."

The Rest of the Story

Coaching comes easy for Chris Petersen. Giving clear responses to the media when asked to explain the Broncos' winning consistency appears much more difficult for him. "Sometimes when you are doing well it's hard to explain or put your finger on it, just as it is when you're not doing well," Petersen told ESPN. "But the bottom line is that we have been fortunate to have success and the kids just really believe they are going to have success and sometimes that's half the battle."

Coach Pete's modesty is commendable, but the "success" Boise State has enjoyed is as much attributable to him as any other person since 2001. As the offensive coordinator and/or head coach, he has been one of the principal designers and overseers of Bronco football success since he joined the staff. The shift and motion offensive schemes introduced by Petersen are not easily learned and take a great deal of individual study and repetition in practice. One of the biggest accomplishments by Petersen and his assistant coaches may be their ability to motivate the offensive players to study and practice what must seem to them a tedious task just to attempt to deceive defenses.

Boise State players, as offensive line Coach Scott Huff expresses it, are called to "buy into" the culture. Buying in essentially translates to maximum personal preparation (weight training, summer practice, playbook and video study), believing what the coaches tell you will work, following their direction, and never considering the individual as more important than the team. This could be the mantra for any major college team in America, but the difference at Boise State appears to be that the players actually believe it and hold each other accountable to assure it is followed by every member of the team.

Another phrase that is thrown around repeatedly by players to describe each other is, "He has a chip on his shoulder." The statement is more than a cliché and may likely be the result of genuine feelings of being underappreciated as prep or junior college prospects. Since the program moved to Division I, the majority of the players making Boise State their choice as a place to play college football was due to the fact they didn't have many, if any other available options.

Former All-American running back Ian Johnson, and the recent face of Bronco football, told Sports Illustrated reporter Arash Markazi after the Fiesta Bowl, "We're all second chance guys. None of us were big-time guys in high school. We understand where everyone on this team is coming from. We look at each other and we all know what it was like to get here. It was tough. When I got recruited by Boise State I had barely even heard of them. I didn't know [anything] about them."

Finally, it's quite possible that no one could have expressed the Boise State mindset better than three-year starter and 2008 senior All-WAC offensive left tackle for Fresno State, Bobby Lepori. Lepori told a reporter at The Fresno Bee, "The number one thing that Boise does is—it's team over individual. And that is so apparent when they're on the football field. You just have people that are selfless. They don't care if they get a stat. They don't care if they get their name in the paper." Lepori goes on, "Honestly, watching them on film is like watching a machine. There's never a mistake. They're never off beat. They just do a great job. In '06, those guys knew what we were doing," he says. "Well before we even snapped a ball, they were calling out our formations, calling our plays. That doesn't come from our bad play calling; that comes from hours and hours and hours of film study. Kids just don't dedicate themselves the way that Boise does."

Twister

Since mid-majors don't operate under the same equal opportunity recruiting process as the majors do, they must often gamble on high school players who switch positions between seasons or are injured in their sophomore or junior years. George Iloka is one of those interesting cases where it was difficult for college coaches to assess his skills.

Iloka, from Kempner High School in Sugar Land, Texas, a suburb of Houston, was a tall, gangly, 6 foot 3, 194-pound wide receiver through his junior year. The new head coach for the 2007 season decided he was better suited for the defensive secondary and moved him to safety before his senior season. Iloka was a very good athlete and several mid-majors indicated some interest, but none offered a scholarship.

Boise State decided to take a gamble and tendered an offer in the summer before Iloka's senior year, even though they had never seen him play defense in a game. TCU, another school with interest, decided the risk was not worth taking and stood on their original offer of a walk-on opportunity.

Iloka immediately gave a verbal (Rice University also made an offer) commitment and then surprised the Bronco staff by informing them that he would graduate in December and enroll at Boise State in January.

Iloka blew onto "The Blue" like a south Texas twister in the Broncos' 2008 spring practice. He learned so quickly that by fall camp it was a forgone conclusion that he would play in his true freshman year.

By the second game, against Bowling Green, Iloka was inserted into the defense in passing situations and then was thrown into the proverbial fire as a starter against nationally ranked Oregon the following week.

Iloka started every game thereafter, ended the season fourth in tackles with 63, and tied for second with four interceptions. Phil Steele, who annually picks his FBS freshman All-American team, listed Iloka as a second team member, joining first-teamer quarterback Kellen Moore and second-team member defensive tackle Billy Winn, two more precocious Broncos.

What makes Iloka's accomplishments even more significant is the fact that he was considered worthy of only a two-star rating under the "athlete" classification. Though some will often move to wide receiver, most players categorized as athletes will play one of the defensive back positions in college. *Rivals.com* listed ninety prospects as athletes (three five-stars, thirty-one four-stars and fifty-six three-stars) for the 2008 class. Iloka's two-star rating didn't warrant ranking so his name did not appear on the list.

True freshman George Iloka was one of only 12 mid-major players of the 54 total (one of three Broncos), to make Phil Steele's Freshman All-American first or second team, while none of the other ninety players ranked ahead of him as "athletes" made either team as a defensive back, wide receiver or any other position.

THEY'RE NO BOISE STATE

The University of South Florida, with its dramatic emergence onto the college football scene, has drawn comparisons to Boise State. USF only began playing Division IAA football in 1997, moved up to D-I in 2001 as an independent, and then in 2003 joined Conference USA. In 2005, they made a leap to the BCS Big East Conference.

When the Bulls rose to a number two ranking in a national poll during the 2007 season, following impressive early season wins over West Virginia and

Auburn, one nationally known commentator stated, "They're no Boise State." He admitted that the reference contained both an off-handed compliment and a put-down of the Broncos.

USF's meteoric rise to prominence is a great story, but when drawing comparisons to Boise State one must put the differences between the two programs into perspective. First, the University of South Florida was already the third-largest university in the state with 40,000 students (nearly twice the size of BSU today) when the football program began.

Though USF was forced to start from scratch with the recruiting process, Florida has a population of 18 million to Idaho's 1.5 million, and only Texas and California rival the state for football talent. With an abundance of quality prospects in Florida, USF has lured 85 percent of its scholarship recruits from the home state, while only about 14 percent of BSU's players have come from Idaho over the same period.

The level of talent, as measured by the recruiting services, is also at a higher level for USF, allowing them to be at or near the average for player quality within the Big East Conference. According to *Rivals.com,* in the seven recruiting years between 2002 and 2008, USF recruited fifty-two blue chip players, including five four-stars and one five-star, while BSU had twenty-four three-stars and one four-star.

It might also be worth mentioning that Boise State has employed five different head coaches since the program moved to D-I in 1996, which is four more than USF. In 2009, Jim Leavitt began his thirteenth consecutive season as the Bulls head coach, allowing the program to maintain a consistency in philosophy that also helps the coaching staff coax recruits to choose USF over other schools.

USF deserves some accolades for its rapid development into a quality program, but since 2001 and through 2008, while Boise State was dominating its conference with six championships, playing in seven bowl games and winning 85 percent of its games, the Bulls had no conference championships, participated in four bowl games and won 63 percent of their games (in fairness, USF defeated all nine of its mid-major opponents in 2002 as an independent). In 2003, Boise State defeated TCU in a bowl game on the Horned Frogs' home field; USF lost to the same team at home. In 2004, an undefeated BSU took Louisville to the final seconds in a four-point Liberty Bowl loss; USF lost to the Cardinals during the regular season by thirty-two.

The University of South Florida may not be "a Boise State" but it seems reasonable to conclude that both schools have succeeded equally in their infancies and early development years as FBS participants—BSU in its economy of mid-majors, through incredible consistency and a flare for occasional overachievement, and precocious USF in its domain, with a penchant for upsetting some giant establishment teams.

Where do they Rank?

Few can argue that over the past ten years Boise State has created a culture where they identify and develop mid-major average recruits, provide them with a system in which they can flourish, and then vastly outperform the market. For good or for bad, the debate will always rage around where the Broncos' season-ending rankings place them in a true competitive sense with the rest of the top 25.

Celebrating a dominant victory over Oregon in the 2009 season-opener, Bronco bloggers could finally throw some convincing statistics at the "overrated" label pinned on them by some of their detractors. Boise State was now 4–1 in its most recent five games against BCS conference teams.

ESPN color commentator Bob Davie stoked the effervescent debate when he suggested during the Oregon game that BSU teams would be hard-pressed to equal their recent win-loss records if they were faced with a dose of BCS conference teams on a weekly basis. A cursory study of the recruiting databases, and even the most loyal of Bronco fans would be sobered by the historical wide gap in prospect values between Boise State and even the most recent bottom-dwelling Pac-10 teams (see Chapter 7).

Before the discussion becomes too hot and heavy a more worthy endeavor might be to evaluate Boise State by first comparing the Broncos' record to that of other top mid-major programs. A look at the winning percentages of the next nine non-BCS universities since 1999 reveals that the Broncos have significantly separated themselves from the rest of the field. Numbers two through ten best winning percentages from highest to lowest of mid-majors are as follows: TCU .73983, Utah .70248, Hawaii .63359, BYU .62903,

Fresno State .62308, Toledo .61157, Southern Miss. .60800, Marshall .59350, and Bowling Green .57143. Boise State has a collective record against seven of these teams of 23–4 over the past ten years, only losing to current fellow conference members Hawaii (2) and Fresno State (1) and TCU in the 2008 Poinsettia Bowl. The Broncos have been victorious over TCU once and Bowling Green, BYU, Southern Miss., and Utah twice each.

BSU president, Bob Kustra, has been lobbying the Mountain West Conference for entry almost from the day he arrived on campus in July of 2003. The political entanglements involving adding teams to fairly static conferences like the MWC are many and varied, even if it seems that the addition of Boise State would at least be geographically sensible. In 2009, MWC Commissioner Craig Thompson admitted that the topic of expansion came up during summer media days, but it was discussed only in generalities. Kustra has received a very cool reception from the MWC in the past, and though a monkey has been known to fall out of a tree occasionally, it appears unlikely there will be changes any time soon.

BSU's 10–1 record against a cross section of MWC teams since 1998 is a solid barometer of the quality the BSU program brings to Division I, especially since many college football analysts consider the MWC to be the best of all the mid-major conferences. It's also conceivable that Boise State could have won a few MWC championships since 1999.

The Broncos began the series in 1998 when they beat a good 7–3 Utah team, following that up the next two years with a win over MWC co-champion Utah in 1999 (a team that included future Pro-Bowl wide receiver Steve Smith and the 2000 NFL Rookie of the Year, running back Mike Anderson) and back-to-back wins over New Mexico.

In seasons '02 through '04 BSU, with a record of 37–3, was so dominant (only losses to BCS Arkansas and Oregon State and future BCS and number seven ranked Louisville) that it is not at all inconceivable they could have won the MWC in at least one and maybe even two of the three years. During that period, they beat Wyoming and BYU twice each by combined scores of 146–69, and also scored a 2002 win over Fresno State by a forty-six point margin, who in turn had beaten the MWC champions, Colorado State, in the same year. Finally, in 2006, the undefeated Broncos bested Wyoming in Laramie and then overran eventual bowl-qualifying Utah in Salt Lake City.

For ten consecutive seasons, Boise State has averaged more than ten wins and less than one loss per year against non-BCS competition it is suited to play every week, dominating its two conferences, and consistently winning against a cross section of intersectional, mid-major opponents. The Broncos are the only mid-major since 2002 and through 2008 to be ranked in the top twenty-five of a national poll five different years at the end of the season. With this kind of success there is, or should be, scant disagreement that Boise State is a worthy candidate for the dominant mid-major program in America for the past ten years.

As for overall performance, detractors will always point to the 6–11 record against BCS teams since 1999 and through the 2009 regular season. Six of the eleven losses occurred between years '99 and '02, and five were road games. Since the end of '02 with a victory over Iowa State in the Humanitarian Bowl, and through the 2009 regular season, the Broncos were 6–5 against BCS competition.

At least some measurement of Boise State's more recent competitiveness with quality BCS teams may be derived from the home-and-home series of consecutive games with Oregon State beginning in 2003 and ending in 2006. The Broncos won both home games in routs, 53–34 and 42–14, while OSU won both home games in struggles, 26–24 and 30–27. In the first game of the series in Corvallis, a highly questionable call by Pac-10 officials favored the Beavers; in their second home game, OSU came from behind to win with less than two minutes left.

These were not mediocre OSU teams by any rationale, but teams with a combined win/loss record of 30–20 overall and 18–15 in the Pac-10. The Beavers generated bowl victories over Notre Dame ('04) and Missouri ('06), along with regular season wins over USC in '06 and Oregon in '04 and '06 when they lost to BSU. From seasons '03 through '06, only fellow Pac-10 members, USC and Cal, won more games.

The strong showing against Oregon State demonstrated that Boise State's blue collar brigade could manage quite well against a program with collectively higher-rated players. For the years '02 through

'06, *Rivals* ranked OSU's five recruiting classes from a best number twenty-six to a worst fifty-two, while BSU received class rankings from number sixty-four to 101. A comparison of blue chip players recruited by each team during the period gives an even more dramatic picture; OSU had sixty-eight three-star or better recruits, while BSU numbered thirteen.

In more recent years, college football writers, commentators, and bloggers have criticized Boise State for not scheduling more BCS teams in non-conference games. The argument (and a reasonable one) is that the Broncos need to prove themselves by playing better competition, if they expect to be chosen for one of the BCS bowl games, even after an undefeated regular season.

By rule the BCS was obligated in 2008 to choose only one non-BCS conference team if that team met the criteria for bowl selection. Utah was the logical choice, since the Utes enjoyed the highest BCS ranking of all non-BCS teams at the end of the regular season. Boise State, however, also met the standards and was ranked only three places below Utah at ninth in the regular season ending poll. The Fiesta Bowl committee made it abundantly clear that even though the Broncos were qualified under the rules for selection, they were not considered a worthy participant. A win over another BCS team besides Oregon during the regular season would almost assuredly have put BSU over the top, but was it worth the risk of scheduling a potential loss?

Athletic director Gene Bleymaier has found a formula allowing his teams to play non-conference mid-major competition to which the Broncos are comparable in player quality. He likely reasons that winning the game against a quality BCS team, coupled with an unblemished record over the balance of the season, is enough to give Boise State a reasonable chance at a marquee bowl game. A BCS bowl bid after an undefeated season, including a blowout win by the Broncos against a good Oregon State team in 2006, would seem to validate his strategy.

Scheduling is more than simply mapping out a strategy to pad the win column; it also involves finding matchups that will help balance the football budget. Boise State is no different than almost every other mid-major program in America with a small stadium and limits on receipts from home games, even with capacity crowds. Bleymaier admitted in the summer of 2009 that the economy forced him to reshuffle and schedule a $1.25 million payday against Atlantic Coast Conference powerhouse Virginia Tech at 92,000-seat FedEx Field, the Landover, Maryland home of the Washington Redskins, in October of 2010. This is likely only the first of many trips to the mid-west or Eastern Time zones to cash in on the rewards available to mid-majors willing to travel to BCS programs with large stadiums, but without reciprocal home game agreements.

While he continues to negotiate with additional BCS conference teams for games in future seasons, Bleymaier's immediate response to the call for better non-conference competition is to schedule a series of concurrent home-and-home games against Mountain West standouts Utah and BYU beginning in 2011.

These are sensible matchups with minimal travel distance requirements and an almost guarantee for higher quality opponents. They also fit into a more aggressive BCS schedule, especially one that may involve trips to the east coast.

Much has been publicized about Fresno State's commitment to play an upgraded non-conference schedule. Since 2001, when Boise State joined the WAC, and through 2008, FSU has played regular season games against twenty-one BCS teams. Many consider the scheduling noble, but the tactic has yet to bring the Bulldogs a conference championship since Boise State entered the WAC. It's debatable whether games against major programs produce a greater toll in injuries, but the emotional and physical demands of traveling to sixteen of the twenty-one games had to wear on players and coaches.

During a 2008 ESPN broadcast of a Boise State game, announcer Rod Gilmore commented, "The Broncos win the games they are supposed to win." The reference was in part to the lower quality of the teams at the bottom half of the WAC. The Western Athletic Conference will never be confused with the SEC or, for that matter, the Pac-10, in terms of overall player quality. As mentioned before, the prospect rankings for all teams in the WAC are well below those of the majority of BCS conference teams, validated each year with the lopsided advantage in wins by majors over conference members.

The seemingly easy conference schedule has not, however, carried over to diminished performances in bowl games since 1999. With the exception of the non-bowl invitation year of 2001, when an 8–4 record and a second place finish in the WAC would have easily qualified them for a bowl game today, the Broncos have more than held their own with a five-win four-loss record and some very exciting games. Five of six bowl games from 2003 to 2008 pitted them against nationally ranked teams at the end of the bowl season. The four losses, Louisville (44–40), Boston College (27–21), East Carolina (41–38), and TCU (17–16), were nail biters that Boise State had every possibility of winning as the final seconds ticked off the game clock.

Boise State, BYU, TCU, and Utah enjoy excellent coaching, and all have proven in recent years that they can produce teams capable of winning consistency. BSU's '07 and '09 recruit class rankings have moved them closer to those of the other three and should provide better player quality and much needed depth for future teams. It seems reasonable to conclude that Boise State is not only very well placed to find itself in the hunt for a BCS bowl game in the foreseeable future, but also in a position to produce teams of the quality to make a very good showing should they be selected.

Leatherheads

One doesn't normally think of Canada as a hotbed for blue chip high school football players. In fact, the farther north from the American border the less football is played. There are, however, some regions of that country where football is very popular and it's not at all unusual to find a few prospects with FBS talent.

Boise State defensive line coach Pete Kwiatkowski got wind of a player from Catholic Central High School in Windsor, Ontario, by the name of Tyrone Crawford, who appeared to have the tools to play major college football. Windsor is not some remote Canadian outpost, but rather a city with a metro population of 320,000, only a five minute drive across the river from the city of Detroit.

Crawford definitely met the coach's expectations on the football field, but he needed to take care of some academic issues before he made the jump to a four-year program. Since it appeared that Crawford would be a non-qualifier, his high school coach, Jalil Khoury, suggested that Kwiatkowski might want to take a look at another CCHS player.

Michael Atkinson was nowhere to be found on the radar screens of the popular recruit information websites for the recruiting season of 2008. In Windsor, Ontario however, he had made quite a name for himself. The 6 foot, 330 pound defensive tackle was his county's defensive player of the year and during his regular high school season he even rushed for 728 yards, picked up another 238 yards in pass receptions and scored seven touchdowns. Kwiatkowski liked what he saw on video and made a late scholarship offer in the spring of 2008.

The Boise State coaches weren't sure what they were getting in Atkinson, but by mid-season as a redshirt on the scout team, the starting offensive linemen gave him the ultimate compliment by affirming that he was tougher to move than any opposing lineman they had faced in games during the season. At season's end, Atkinson picked up the scout team defensive player of the year award, and during the final spring practice Blue & Orange game of 2009, the coaches let him run the ball on two plays. Atkinson displayed some of his high school flash when he took a hand-off and popped outside of an off tackle play for a 25 yard gain.

ESPN's Bruce Feldman was so impressed with Atkinson's performance on the scout team that he named him one of the top 10 transfers, early-enrolled freshmen or redshirts for the pre-season of 2009. Atkinson, who was listed in only one recruiting service database as a one-star and not considered FBS quality in the 2008 recruiting class, was part of Feldman's elite group that included two five-star, five four-star and two three-star prospects.

As for 6 foot 5, 258 pound defensive end, Tyrone Crawford, the original Windsor target for signing by the Boise State coaches, he gave a verbal commitment to the Broncos in the summer of 2009 after an outstanding freshman season at Bakersfield Junior College. With his academic shortcomings resolved to the satisfaction of the coaches, Crawford plans to join the Bronco recruit class of 2010.

WHAT A GREAT PLACE TO LIVE

In July of 2007, Chris Petersen, Ian Johnson and Jared Zabransky traveled to Hollywood, where the trio accepted ESPN ESPY Awards presented to Boise State for "The Best Game" and "The Best Play" of the year in the Fiesta Bowl. By August of 2007, 60,000 DVDs of the Fiesta Bowl had been sold nationally, at least 12,000 more than the number sold of the national championship game. Boise State, with football as essentially the only real national draw, was the highest rated non-BCS school in the Collegiate Licensing

Company's rankings (a position the Broncos still held through the March 2009 fiscal year report by CLC). Before the end of the year, Fiesta Bowl offensive MVP Jared Zabransky found his likeness on the cover of a popular video game. In 2008, *The Best Damned Sports Show in America* named the "hook-and-lateral" and "statue" Fiesta Bowl plays in its top ten of The Best Damn Top 100 Mind Blowing Moments (of all time).

The Future Looks Bright

On flight landing approach to San Diego's Lindberg Field, one can observe an area of greater population than the entire state of Idaho. At 1.5 million, only the states of Alaska, Hawaii, Montana and Wyoming are less populated in the West. Boise's 210,000 people, with an additional 175,000 in Ada County, comprise Idaho's most densely populated metropolitan area. If there was ever any concern that the city's relatively small population could support and follow its mid-major program to a BCS bowl game, those fears were dispelled when the Bronco Nation easily matched Oklahoma Sooner ticket holders at the Fiesta Bowl.

Demographic studies and population growth statistics show that the Treasure Valley of southwestern Idaho is one of the fastest growing regions in the United States. In 2008, *Forbes Magazine* rated Boise the second best of two hundred metro areas in the country for business and careers. Farmers Insurance, in its 2006 listing of most secure places in America, rated Boise number one, and in the same year *Money*

Magazine ranked Boise number eight as the best place to live. These are positive signs for the city, university, and football program. With dynamic population growth, especially of the variety that has plenty of disposable income, the financial backing for Boise State football should be on a secure footing for years to come.

There is no question that the community has established its place in the football success equation. "I think a lot of [Boise State's success] has to do with the fan support here," head coach Petersen commented. "Everybody knows it's very important, the university has always thought it's very important. It's just kind of always worked. And then once you have that tradition and expectations, everybody works very hard to carry out the mission."

Large, boisterous crowds are a big draw for recruits when they make official visits during the season to attend games or watch them on television. In the West, other than Boise State, only a handful of the teams in the WAC and MWC fill their stadiums to capacity for most home games. The western mid-major teams are not the only ones to have difficulty putting bodies in the seats. For example, when the Mid-American Conference was producing BCS-killer teams in 2003, average attendance for home games for the conference was less than 20,000.

In the fall of 2008, Bronco Stadium's capacity of 30,000 was increased by about 1,550 premium seats with the addition of the six-story, 136,000-square-foot, $36 million Stueckle Sky Center, which includes luxury suites and a-state-of-the-art press box. All but one suite and a few individual seats were left unsold prior to the '08 opening game. In the summer of 2009, a new field seating structure was installed in the south end zone adding an additional 1,500 seats bringing total stadium capacity to more than 33,000. The administration is anticipating that the overall demand will be high enough for tickets that plans are in place to eventually add an additional 10,000 to 15,000 seats, as funding is available.

BSU routinely fills the stadium to capacity for home games and could easily sell several thousand more tickets for the most attractive matchups. There were 21,000 season-ticket holders at the end of the 2008 season, not counting the Stueckle Sky Club (another 1,550 seats), and a waiting list for an additional 3,500 seats.

Boise State has also committed to improving the football infrastructure to bring practice facilities to the level of those in the top Mountain West Conference universities. In February of 2006, the $9.5 million Caven-Williams Sports Complex, a 78,000 square foot field house, opened. With Boise's chilly falls, cold winters and unpredictable springs, the indoor facility was a functional and recruiting necessity. If one considers the number of players from Southern California alone, the warm confines of an indoor practice venue could be the difference between luring a three-star and a two-star prospect.

What part has the media played in the success of Boise State football? ESPN and Boise State created a mutual admiration society dating back to the Broncos' 1999 Humanitarian Bowl win over Louisville in that network's most watched bowl game of the 1999/2000 season. The partnership through various conference and bowl televised game agreements has proved to be extremely beneficial to both parties—BSU with the opportunity to showcase the football program nationally, ESPN with some highly rated non-BCS games. During the 2004 season with six nationally televised regular season games, including four at home and two on the road, BSU had better coverage than a large number of BCS programs The national exposure, an undefeated regular season, and a Liberty Bowl appearance that year undoubtedly helped attract BSU's highest rated recruiting class to that point in 2005.

It is also apparent that the Fiesta Bowl win gave a solid boost to 2007 recruiting fortunes. One blue chip prospect, Hunter White, a linebacker from Huntington Beach, California, was so excited about the bowl win that he called coach Petersen's cell phone after the Fiesta Bowl game during the Broncos' team bus ride back to the hotel to make his verbal commitment.

Giving evidence to the excellent recruiting class, four true freshmen position players and a punter were brought up at the start of the '07 season. The three offensive players, wide receivers Austin Pettis and Titus Young, along with running back D. J. Harper, earned significant playing time and accounted for ninety-three pass receptions, 1,291 yards from scrimmage (480 rushing, 811 pass receiving), and seventeen touchdowns.

It is unlikely that Boise State will ever find itself in a position where elite players will be knocking down the door to get in, but it appears that a significant change is brewing in the program's efforts to upgrade the quality of its recruits. With notoriety from ten years of sustained success, the Bronco coaching staff is able to make scholarship offers to higher rated players and expect some to sign.

It is also evident that the Broncos can now go toe to toe with the Pac-10 and the MWC in the race to elicit early verbal commitments. Ten prospects from the 2009 recruiting class, all but two commanding three-star ratings or more from *Rivals* and/or *Scout*, had given verbal commitments to Boise State before the end of July, 2008. By contrast, only three verbal commitments were made by the same time in '07 for the 2008 class. According to *Scout.com,* of the Division I schools in the eleven Western States, only USC, UCLA, and BYU received more verbal commitments by the last day of July, 2008.

Higher ranking recruits from the western states who just two or three years ago would likely have accepted a scholarship from a lower level Pac-10 team or a MWC member are, instead, choosing Boise State. Joe Southwick, a nationally top twenty-five-ranked quarterback from Northern California's East Bay area in the Broncos' 2009 class, was philosophical when he assessed his chances of being part of a team with a 12–0 regular season and possible BCS bowl game bid were greater at BSU than they would be at a low to mid-level Pac-10 program.

The 2009 recruit class appears to be exceptional by all indications, but Boise State's football coaches might be advised to maintain their ten-year, well-tested philosophy of finding blue collar players. In the 2009 spring practice session, only a handful of players were singled out by Coach Pete for superlatives. They included a pair of walk-ons without scholarships, and another scholarship player judged by the recruiting services as unworthy of a Division I rating. One of those walk-ons, Michael Ames, was a twenty-two year-old redshirt freshman who hadn't played football in a real game since high school. He was so impressive in the spring and fall camps that offensive line coach Scott Huff picked him as the 2009 season-opening game starter at offensive right tackle.

Less than two weeks after the 2009 BCS national championship game was played, Stewart Mandel of *Sports Illustrated* made his top-twenty predictions for the fall college football season. His selection for the tenth position was Boise State, the highest placement for any non-BCS team.

Mandel suggested that five players would be instrumental in leading the Broncos to another possible BCS bowl game—sophomore quarterback Kellen Moore, junior defensive end Ryan Wynterswyk, senior cornerback Kyle Wilson, junior safety Jeron Johnson, and junior running back Jeremy Avery. Probably not surprisingly, every player fits the mold of an overachiever so typical of many past Boise State recruits.

Moore was the lone player among the five Bronco prospects out of high school to be judged a blue chip, garnering three stars from *Rivals* but ranked thirty-first of all pro-style quarterbacks. Only Notre Dame's Jimmy Clausen (a true sophomore in '08 with a previous year's experience), the number one ranked quarterback (and the overall number one rated player) in the country for the '07 recruit class, came close to matching Moore's passing statistics in 2008. Clausen's 132.5 passing efficiency rating was well below Moore's 157.1, and Moore had three hundred more passing yards (3,486 to 3,172) and a better pass completion ratio (281–405 vs. 268–440)—both threw twenty-five touchdown passes. Just a handful of the other twenty-nine quarterbacks ranked ahead of Moore in the '07 high school class threw more than one hundred completions in '08 and Jarrett Lee from LSU was by far the most successful. However, Lee's efficiency rating of 116.9 (eighty-first, compared to Moore's twelfth place ranking) paled next to Moore's.

Winterswyk, a member of the preliminary watch list for the 2009 Lombardi Award, given to the nation's best down lineman, didn't even appear on any of the recruiting services' radar screens when he graduated from high school in 2005. He was a walk-on in 2006 and wasn't even sure what position he would play until 2007.

Wilson, from New Jersey, a 2009 preseason Playboy Magazine All-American pick and *Rivals.com's* selection as the number thirty-two ranked player in college football, was a two-star recruit holding only a pair of FBS scholarship offers outside of Boise State. In the 2005 recruiting class *Rivals* listed sixty-nine cornerbacks with ratings of three stars or more; Wilson was not among them.

Johnson was a 5 foot 11, 175 pound two-star high school linebacker from Southern California who was thought by some to lack the speed and size to play anywhere in the secondary. Avery, a 5 foot 9, 160-pound running back without a listing in any of the recruiting service databases, was offered a scholarship after BSU coaches traveled to his Los Angeles area high school to recruit another player. He received no other D-I offers and was considering D-IAA Eastern Washington University.

After the ten-year run of success enjoyed by Boise State, the expectation might be for at least a little bit more star power than this group generates. However, that just doesn't fit the blue collar model for Boise State football.

e|LIVE

listen|imagine|view|experience

AUDIO BOOK DOWNLOAD INCLUDED WITH THIS BOOK!

In your hands you hold a complete digital entertainment package. Besides purchasing the paper version of this book, this book includes a free download of the audio version of this book. Simply use the code listed below when visiting our website. Once downloaded to your computer, you can listen to the book through your computer's speakers, burn it to an audio CD or save the file to your portable music device (such as Apple's popular iPod) and listen on the go!

How to get your free audio book digital download:

1. Visit www.tatepublishing.com and click on the e|LIVE logo on the home page.
2. Enter the following coupon code:
   4058-38d4-6a62-a5b8-9d82-d765-b472-0059
3. Download the audio book from your e|LIVE digital locker and begin enjoying your new digital entertainment package today!